D0948316

TWAYNE'S WORLD AUTHORS SERIES
A Survey of the World's Literature

FRANCE

Maxwell A. Smith, Guerry Professor of French, Emeritus
The University of Chattanooga
Former Visiting Professor in Modern Languages
The Florida State University
EDITOR

Fernand Crommelynck

TWAS 444

Fernand Crommelynck

FERNAND CROMMELYNCK

By BETTINA L. KNAPP

Hunter College
and the Graduate Center of the
City University of New York

TWAYNE PUBLISHERS

A DIVISION OF G. K. HALL & CO., BOSTON

Copyright © 1978 by G. K. Hall & Co.
All Rights Reserved
First Printing

Library of Congress Cataloging in Publication Data

Knapp, Bettina Liebowitz, 1926–
    Fernand Crommelynck.

    (Twayne's world authors series ; TWAS 444 :
France)
    Bibliography: p. 155–57
    Includes index.
    1. Crommelynck, Fernand, 1888–1970—Criticism and
Interpretation.
PQ2605.R76Z75   842'.9'12   77-22465
ISBN 0-8057-6286-8

MANUFACTURED IN THE UNITED STATES OF AMERICA

"Nothing is funnier than unhappiness . . .
Yes, yes, it's the most comical thing
in the world."

(Samuel Beckett, *Endgame*)

Contents

About the Author

Bettina L. Knapp is Professor of Romance Languages and Comparative Literature at Hunter College and the Graduate Center of CUNY. She received her B.A. from Barnard and her M.A. and Ph.D. from Columbia. She also studied at the Sorbonne. She is the author of *Louis Jouvet, Man of the Theatre: Louise Labé; Le Mirliton*, a novel based on the life of Aristide Bruant; *Antonin Artaud Man of Vision; Jean Genet: Jean Racine, Mythos and Renewal in Modern Theatre; Céline Man of Hate; Off-Stage Voices*, twenty-eight interviews with French dramatists, actors, and directors; *French Writers Speak Out*, interviews with French novelists: *Gérard de Nerval, The Mystic's Dilemma*. She is co-author of *That was Yvette* and translator of *Cymbalum Mundi*. She has published articles in *La Revue D'Histoire du Théâtre; Yale/Theatre; Yale French Studies; Kentucky Romance Quarterly; Drama and Theatre; Show; Nineteenth-Century French Studies; Dada and Surrealism; Books Abroad; French Review; Comparative Drama*, etc. Dr. Knapp is the recipient of a Guggenheim Fellowship and of a Grant from the American Philosophical Society. She is presently at work on a volume to be entitled *The Promethean Myth*.

Preface

Crommelynck's theater is neither a civic festival nor a morality lesson, nor is it designed for relaxation. It is a theater of action, of psychological probings, of character evolution, of dramatic climaxes, and of shattering suspense scenes. The bizarre machinations of his protagonists, their instinctuality and crudeness, bring to mind the seventeenth-century farceurs. The young Molière, it has been claimed, had been attracted to the Pont-Neuf to observe the antics and verbal routines of the famous Tabarin, who would abash his viewers with his exaggerated visual and auditive compositions. Just as Turlupin and Gros-Guillaume used to perform their acrobatic and clowning feats, their jokes, and their seemingly unlimited repertoire, so Crommelynck's imagination ripples along. He captures the rudimentary temperament of the farceurs in *The Magnificent Cuckold* and *Golden Tripe*; and the lithe and imaginative quality of the *commedia dell'arte* plays with their *zanni* ways and stock characters in *Carine*; the hermetic implications of the mask in *The Sculptor of Masks*; the symbolic and illusory realm in *The Puerile Lovers*; the more popular blends of boulevard theater in *Hot and Cold* and in *A Woman Whose Heart Is too Small*. To the innovations of his forerunners, Crommelynck adds his own spice and ironic overtones. Although Crommelynck's goal is to amuse, he also follows Hamlet's suggestion to the players, "to hold, as 'twere, the mirror up to nature!"

The hilarity of Crommelynck's monstrous emanations is only apparent. The fun lies on the surface; it is a mask with its bent for the macabre and somber, its need for the grotesque, its derisive tendency to debase what is beautiful in life and to destroy the tenuous spiritual climes. Treachery, eroticism, and satiric ferocity are *de rigueur*.

Crommelynck's plays are extraordinary vehicles for the well-trained actor. Throughout *Golden Tripe* and *The Magnificent Cuckold*—a combination of burlesque, mime, puppetry, and grand drama—the performers find themselves in a state of near-perpetual motility. Every now and then, for variety's sake, short moments of repose are offered actor and audience in *Carine* and *Hot and Cold*. The inventiveness required to flesh out the characters, to increase the tension implicit in the situations, and to provoke laughter, is dependent upon the actor's own power of creativity. Because there is little rational connection between the scenes and even the dialogue, the onus of filling the gap, and thus offering viewers some kind of meaningful connection between the sequences of events and moods, falls on the actors. Gestures, therefore, are of the utmost importance, as are vocal techniques, clowning, facial expressions, and alteration of rhythms.

The inner core of Crommelynck's beings is a composite of cruelty and ruthlessness. We are made privy to a dramatist who cuts his characters open; who inflates their traits and ridicules their propensities with carnal delight in the manner of a Hieronymus Bosch, a James Ensor, and many of the German Expressionists, such as Emil Nolde or Egon Schiele. Onstage, therefore, there are beatings and whippings; a series of visual dialectics that divest the happenings of all sensitivity; cacophonies that include raucous speech, screeching, jeering, and snickering. Subtleties, understanding, and tenderness have been banished from Crommelynck's world. We are at the antipodes of Giraudoux's golden realm, of Anouilh's illusory domain, closer to the nightmarish and fiendish ghouls of an Arrabal, Vauthier, or Ghelderode—each wearing the gargoyle's smirk. Crommelynck's theater flagellates in the most spectacular of ways!

BETTINA L. KNAPP

Acknowledgments

My thanks go to the American Philosophical Society for the generous grant they awarded me to further my research work on Fernand Crommelynck's theater. I also owe a debt of gratitude to the Arsenal Library in Paris, the Royal Library in Brussels, and to the New York Public Library for the articles, letters, and books they made available to me. For information concerning productions, acting techniques, and insights into Crommelynck's personality, my appreciation goes to Mme Orgels-Stoumon, editor of *Le Flambeau*; to Roger Blin, who acted Estrugo in *The Magnificent Cuckold*; to Daniel Emilfork, who played Baron Cazou in *The Puerile Lovers*; to Dr. and Mme Ado Avrane, who had seen so many of Crommelynck's plays in those early days and regaled me with their reactions to them; and to Professor Maxwell Smith, a patient and inspiring guide.

Chronology

1954   Translation and adaptation of Shakespeare's *Sir John Falstaff*.
1970   Crommelynck dies at Saint-Germain-en-Laye on March 17.

CHAPTER 1

Introduction

F ERNAND Crommelynck was born in Paris on November 19, 1866. His father was Bourguignon of Belgian ancestry; his mother, French from the Savoyard region. In view of the fact that both his father and his uncle were actors, it is not surprising that the young Crommelynck should have manifested a fascination for the theater early in life. Equal to his passion for the theater was his hatred for formal education. He despised the constraints imposed upon him in the classroom. School was claustrophobic. He preferred roaming through the back streets of his native Montmartre with its cobblestones and its ancient, frequently crumbling, houses. There he observed all types of people, their small joys and sorrows, their rancors and kindnesses. When reminiscing about his neighborhood years later, he alluded to it as one inspiring "silence and solitude." He spoke with affection about his younger years spent "vagabonding" from the rue du Roi d'Alger to his neighborhood school on rue Ferdinand-Flocon, to the place du Tertre with its small theaters and cabarets. It was in these neighborhood theaters that his father used to perform in the popular melodramas of the day.[1]

At the age of twelve Crommelynck left school and took a job at a stockbroker's office. He knew then, however, that his future lay in the theater. Two years later he made his debut at the Bouffes Parisiens. Meanwhile, his father, having inherited some money from his parents, moved to Brussels where he could live comfortably with his family, and the young Crommelynck followed.[2]

Crommelynck had discovered in himself not only a flair for acting, but also for writing. It was this latter talent that he now chose to

15

pursue seriously. By 1906 he could boast of two works in print in a Belgian magazine, *En Art*: "Clématyde," a short story with mystical, gory, and erotic overtones; and the first poetic version of the play *The Sculptor of Masks*. A third work, a dramatic idyll, *We'll Not Go to the Woods Any More*, won the Thyrse prize and was performed at the Théâtre du Parc in Brussels on April 28, 1906.

I   We'll Not Go to the Woods Any More

We'll Not Go to the Woods Any More is a one-act, rustic play written with the enthusiasm and ebullience of youth. Crommelynck's taste for nature in the manner of a Ronsard and a La Fontaine is clearly evident in his glowing imagery and the richness of his emotions. The action takes place in the outskirts of Paris in 1831. Onstage are a white frame house with green shutters, an old tree trunk, lanterns, a garden filled with flowers, and a forest in the distance. On frontstage, Ermessinde, a forty-five-year-old woman and guardian of the eighteen-year-old Fanchette, is sewing. Jerome, fifty years old, is reading a newspaper. Ermessinde begins teasing Jerome, first about his annoying habit of pulling his ear, then about certain differences that have come up concerning finances. However, more distressing is the problem of jealousy. Fanchette enters into the conversation off and on, but spends most of her time daydreaming about her Sylvain. Every night Sylvain comes to the house and leaves a letter for Fanchette in the tree trunk that she picks up, leaving a letter for him in turn. But then, certain evenings, no letters are forthcoming, and the suspense heightens. After some misunderstandings, *quid pro quos*, and strange coincidences, all ends on a happy note. Fanchette marries her Sylvain and Jerome his Ermessinde.

We'll Not Go to the Woods Any More certainly is naive in its use of theatrical conventions and in the stock types it portrays: the little country girl, or ingenue, the young farm boy, the older woman who plays at being guardian, and the older fiancé. However, the naturalness and spontaneity of the dialogue are arresting. Crommelynck's love refrains are discreet and sensitive, stamped with a delicacy of feeling that is reminiscent of certain of La Fontaine's *Tales*. A dream quality also emerges from the dramatic sequences, particularly during Fanchette's and Sylvain's poignant monologues. These passages remind one of Honoré d'Urfé's *L'Astrée*, where, during the dream, the lovers abandon themselves to each other in the most refined way. *We'll Not Go to the Woods Any More* is a modern pastoral comedy; as in Racan's *Bergeries*, gentleness and wisdom are opposed to unabashed passion. In 1907 Crommelynck wrote *To Each his Own*. This one-act prose play was printed in the *Revue Générale* in Brussels, but to our knowledge it has never been performed.

II *Influence of Verhaeren and Others*

The theater was not Crommelynck's only interest. His father, who loved to recite verse—as do so many French actors—instilled in his son a love for poetry. Thus, it comes as no surprise that Crommelynck committed many poems to memory. His favorite authors were Hugo, Musset, Baudelaire, Laforgue, and—the one to become his master above all—Emile Verhaeren, the author of *The Flemings, Hallucinated Countrysides, Tentacular Cities,* and *Dawns.* Verhaeren expressed "the coarse, brutal, tumultuous aspect of Flemish character,"[3] and rejected the macabre and the abnormal, characteristics so popular in Flemish literature: "No more morbid subjects. No more fake mysticism. But strong characters who make sparks fly in conflict."[4] His powerful style, agnostic mysticism, Mallarméan Symbolism, and bent for Naturalism with its focus on the sordid side of life attempted to arouse "sensations and feelings in the spectator."[5] Verhaeren was convinced that, through the work of art and through his own willpower, the individual could transcend the sorrows of his life. In *Dawns* he delineated the gruesome nature of war, arousing in his viewers a spirit of revolt against any government that would impose a conflagration upon its people. When Meyerhold produced *Dawns* in Moscow, he interpreted it as a "proletarian revolution against imperialism and militarism."[6]

Verhaeren's influence on Crommelynck the poet is quite obvious. Verhaeren's sharp, abrasive imagery in depicting the modern industrial age with its enormous machines—powerful enough to crush man and annihilate any potential for individualism—his social idealism, and his understanding of human nature did much to expand Crommelynck's outlook on life and deepen his own views.

Verhaeren's style is also discernible in some of Crommelynck's short stories, as in "Clématydes," incisively written but with a definite penchant for gore and brutality; in "The House of Owls," equally powerful in its sharp and cutting representations but with Crommelynck's own violent bent, whereas "The Hurricane" demonstrates a breaking away from the master and a more original turn of events. In "The Hurricane," Crommelynck broaches what are to become his favorite themes; jealousy, cuckoldry, and murderous instincts. [7]

On April 29, 1908, Crommelynck married the daughter of a café owner in Brussels, Anna-Marie Joséphine Letellier. The young couple made their home first in Brussels, then in Ostend, and finally in Paris.

In Ostend Crommelynck met James Ensor, whose paintings were to have a strong effect upon his imagination. The use of the mask, the power of the grotesque, and the self-inflicted torture implicit in Ensor's canvases struck a sympathetic note in Crommelynck. In the later versions of the Sculptor of Masks as well as in The Puerile Lovers and in The Merchant of Regrets macabre and surreal creatures prevail. Goya's monstrous and mad-faced beings as etched in Los Caprichos coupled with the violence of his bullfighting scenes must also have impressed Crommelynck. The boldness of Goya's satire, the terrifying buffoons with their fantastic deformities, seemed to add to Crommelynck's already tormented nature. Also influential on the young playwright were the works of Tolstoi and Dostoevski. Interestingly, the first version of The Sculptor of Masks was performed in Moscow in 1906. [8]

Crommelynck conceived The Merchant of Regrets when he was only eighteen years old. Its first production took place at the Théâtre du Parc in Brussels (1913); its second, which won acclaim, was directed by Georges Pitoëff at the Théâtre des Arts in Paris (1927). Pitoëff asked Mme C. P. Simon to compose a musical score for his production. She chose soft, light, and rippling tonal sequences in the manner of Debussy's Pelléas and Mélisande, in which recitatives and orchestral accompaniments were ingeniously interwoven. The Pitoëff production marked two other events: Ludmilla Pitoëff, the director's wife, made her singing debut, and Vladimir Golschmann won accolades for his conducting. According to the critics, Mme Pitoëff sang the lead in a most enchanting way, captivating the spectators with the ease in which she blended her graceful acting and melodious singing. Of Golschmann, Georges Pitoëff stated prophetically: "He is a young orchestra leader with a great future."[9]

III   The Merchant of Regrets

The Merchant of Regrets takes place in a foggy city during the Middle Ages. An old antique dealer has married a beautiful young girl. But she is unhappy because she feels he is in love with "the skeletons of his past" and not with her. He lives with his dusty old furniture, his clocks, gold chasubles, skulls, Christ figures, rugs, porcelains, military equipment, and stuffed monkeys. He stands for egoism and an undue attachment to the past. When he does talk to his wife, it is always in connection with some old relic.

I must see Monsieur le Curé. I think I'll get him the great cross of calvary—you know? The great cross which was discovered in Palestine, way down beneath the earth. It's worm-eaten. It's really the true cross of God.

To which is wife answers:

"Jesus died in the wind, on two crossed branches."

The antique dealer cannot understand why his wife becomes progressively more detached. He is unaware of the fact that she needs light, life, and love. Claude, the village miller, fulfills these requirements. Claude and the girl leave together, thanks to the intervention of a neighbor who is depicted as a demoniacal, witchlike shrew. She taunts the old man after his wife's departure and calls him "cuckold." He is so outraged that he kills her and accuses the village idiot of the murder. The wife returns, after having kissed her lover in broad daylight, while her husband seeks refuge in the shadows.

Although the plot is rather puerile, the germ of Crommelynck's future work is present: his themes of unrequited love, misun-

derstandings, antitheses between youth and age; his salient and
individualistic characterizations of the charming wife, the demoniacal neighbor, the village idiot; and the earthiness and lyricism
of the dialogue. More important, however, are Crommelynck's
ferocity, acerbic humor, and penchant for the grotesque, which—
still in an embryonic stage—emerge in solidly delineated contours.

Georges Pitoëff, a visionary in the directing field whose sensitivity and imaginative powers gave France H.-R. Lenormand's *The
Time is a Dream,* Chekhov's *Uncle Vania,* and Ibsen's *Enemy of the
People* (to mention but a few of his productions), was impressed with
The Merchant of Regrets and his directing was inspired. For Pitoëff
the text was of supreme importance. Whatever the director's designs or techniques, they were to flow naturally from the dramatist's
work. Pitoëff's mise-en-scène was thus a plastic transcription of the
mysterious atmosphere in which the play was bathed; it was an
interplay of delightful and terrorizing sensations. The decor was
ingenious: a large room filled with antiques and a bay window on the
far side that opened into the country, delineating both worlds on
stage—imprisonment within freedom, light in darkness.[10]

In 1916 Crommelynck founded his own acting company in Brussels, which he called the Flying-Theater because it moved about in
the city so frequently, playing in whatever theater was vacant at the
time: the Palais de Glace, the Gaieté, La Scalla, Salle Patria.
Crommelynck offered audiences plays by Ibsen, Tristan Bernard,
Franc-Nohain, and, of course, his own. This gave Crommelynck the
opportunity to become thoroughly acquainted with the theater in
terms of its conventions and aesthetics as well as with the financial
aspects. It was the financial situation that led to the disbanding of
the Flying-Theater in 1918. Yet, the two-year stint had given him an
opportunity to display his own histrionic talents: his diction was
precise, his gestures stylized when necessary, and his lean figure
striking. What was unforgettable was his face: thin lips, narrow but
forceful eyes that usually stared into the distance, and high
cheekbones—a face that wore the expression of a man at odds with
himself and the world.

Crommelynck was present for the Paris production of *The Magnificent Cuckold* (1920), his biggest success—a play which marked a

significant date in the history of the theater; he was also present for
The Puerile Lovers (1921), *Golden Tripe* (1925), *Carine* (1929), *A Woman Whose Heart Is too Small* (1934), and *Hot and Cold* (1934).
Crommelynck spent World War II in comfort in Brussels, as director of the Théâtre des Galeries; and also in occupied Paris.[11]

IV *Revivals During the Occupation*

During the German Occupation several of his plays were revived:
The Magnificent Cuckold at the Théâtre Hébertot (1941), starring Marcel Roels and Roger Blin; *A Woman Whose Heart Is too Small* at the Théâtre de l'Oeuvre (1942), directed by Crommelynck; *Hot and Cold* (renamed *Leona* for the occasion) at the Ambassadeurs, featuring Mme Alice Cocea (1944). After the holocaust the most notable revivals in France were *Carine* (1949), with Jean-Louis Barrault, Madeleine Renaud, and Roger Blin; *Hot and Cold* (1956), starring Jean-Marie Serreau, Claude Gensac, and directed by Crommelynck; *The Puerile Lovers* (1956) with Michel Vitold, Daniel Emilfork, and Tania Balachova who also directed the play.

The majority of the revivals received favorable reviews, but *Hot and Cold* did not. Although Crommelynck had once declared in an article in *Comoedia*[12] that he "observed the discipline of silence, refusing ever to mix into debates with critics," he broke his steadfast rule and entered into the mêlée. He pointed out the ignorance of the reviewers with regard to literature and the arts in general. They always have recourse to labels or to appellations. Because he has a Flemish name, they call his theater "foggy since it emerged from the land of the North." This appellation, he contended, has been used almost continuously since it was given to Ibsen. The North is supposed to be dull and dreary and dark—thus "irrational." Is the French world always to be considered exclusively "logical"? Is their approach always "classically clear"? The same critics who label Flemish painting hazy, cloudy, dull-colored, need only look at the canvases of van Eyck or Rogier van der Weyden or Memling "to see décors painted in azure blue, enamels, and gold. Where are the clouds in Brueghel's canvases, or in those of Rubens, Jordaens, van Dyck? The land of the dukes of Burgundy," he concluded, "burn with their oriflammes . . . The façades of the city and the country houses are illuminated as brilliantly as the *Very Rich Hours* of the Duc de Berry."[13]

V   *Flemish and French Theatrical Traditions*

Crommelynck's theater is a composite of Flemish and French traditions combined with his own personal style.

When speaking of Flemish theater—as one does of Flemish painting—one usually refers to an area extending from Bruges to the coast region from Calais to the Scheldt. In the Middle Ages this area was divided into two parts: the west of Flanders—which included the towns of Bruges, Ostend, Courtrai, Ypres—and the east of Flanders—which included Antwerp, Ghent, and the rich area watered by the Scheldt.

Generally speaking, Flemish characteristics may be described as an attitude of extreme realism toward existence and, paradoxically, a penchant for mysticism. These characteristics were said to have been introduced by the Spaniards during their occupation of this area, but according to J. A. Goris were present long before that time. The Flemish felt a deep-seated need to transcend their workaday world. They yearned for some spiritual realm that would bring them serenity and create unity where there was diversity—in the phenomenological world. They needed the surreal realm of their imaginations to create their masterpieces. Compelled to contend with the rigors of their climate and the multitude of economic difficulties facing a nation surrounded by enemies seeking to divest it of its sovereignty, the Flemish had to deal with reality on solid footing. But Flemish reality must not be confused with French nineteenth-century Naturalism and its attempt to duplicate what the Naturalists saw scientifically in their arts and letters. Flemish reality includes the phenomenological realm as well as the surreal world: fantasy and phantasmagoria, where the logical and intangible cohabit.

Their reality surpasses reason. The Fleming is essentially a man for whom the supernatural exists. Jan van Eyck paints with utmost precision the sumptuous raiment of the Arnolfini, the little dog of the Arnolfini, the precious shoes ready for wear, and the rosary of crystal beads—all these personal objects arranged around the young man and his bride as tokens of security in a quiet, well-ordered home. But he will not forget the convex mirror that opens the room to the outside world, and even to the world of magic. Such is Flemish realism. It opens onto the unknown, on the unusual.[14]

The distinctly Flemish brand of mysticism and realism, of pathos and merrymaking, are expressed most spectacularly in Pieter Brueghel's *The Battle Between Carnival and Lent*. In this canvas, people are crowded together; they are at play. Suddenly, their revelry turns to madness as the long wild night of the Mardi Gras is slowly transformed into the depressing dawn of Ash Wednesday and the beginning of Lent. Two opposing spirits are present in Brueghel's work: the penitent and the carouser; the roisterer and the reveler. In *Peasant Wedding*, another Brueghel canvas, the rustic tables and benches upon which the peasants are seated as they indulge in an abundance of food and drink are crudely depicted and may be compared with the restrained elegance of the city folk—and perhaps their hypocritical ways. Coarseness of feelings (considered another Flemish characteristic), is frequently injected in the tavern scenes depicted by Adriaen Brouwer. Hieronymus Bosch's repulsive and monstrous forms, demons who attack, gape at, and assault the holy man in *The Temptation of St. Anthony*, also inhabit the Flemish soul. The violent and instinctive visions of Maurice de Vlaminck, with their strident reds, blues, greens, their fast and furious rhythms, the harshness of their brushstrokes and explosive qualities of the trees, rivers, and skies, are likewise part of Flemish nature.

These characteristics are also implicit in the Flemish comic tradition of the *sotternyen* ("tomfooleries"), the *boerden* ("comic farces"), and the *klutchten* ("farces") performed during the Middle Ages. These plays brought into focus man's more absurd side and elicited laughter by ridiculing, derogating, profaning, and deforming what was considered sacred: church and state.

The comic tradition in both France and Belgium aroused humor by pointing to man's vices—his cupidity, hypocrisy, and gluttony— sparing no classes from cleric and nun to king and courtier. Comedy

as delineated frequently in the farce destroyed logical order of
things through slapstick humor of all types: interruptions, mis-
pronunciations, profanations, coincidences, catch phrases, quid pro
quos, exaggerated pantomime, or beatings. In all of their deformities, clowns and buffoons represented man's physical imperfec-
tions. But these clowns who aroused laughter in others spoke their
words pointedly in bitter, satirical tones, revealing the deficiencies
in those around them—less obvious, perhaps, but far more insidious.[15]

In more recent centuries Verhaeren, Maeterlinck, van Lerberghe, and Rodenbach continued in the medieval tradition but
introduced new elements. In *Princess Maleine, The Intruder*, and
The Interior, Maeterlinck created a symbolic theater with sparse
language, short scenes, and a mystical frame of reference. Writing
about *Princess Maleine* in *La Jeune Belgique*, Iwan Gilking declared
it to be "an important work which should be considered a landmark
in the history of contemporary theater." Charles van Lerberghe's
The Detectors, which Lugné-Poë directed at the Odéon, could be
labeled a mystery play as well as a symbolic drama because it featured a girl forced to face death—a prominent theme in Flemish and
German literature throughout the Middle Ages.[16] Georges Rodenbach's *The Veil* and *The Miracle* is weighted down with symbolism,
frequently quite obvious: antique bells, candles, crystals, and a
panoply of other objects that encourage a macabre and supernatural
atmosphere. Cyriel Buysse wrote in Flemish but with the
naturalism of a Becque and Zola. His *De Plaatsvervangende Vre-
derechter* was a satire on the judiciary system. Its humor was biting
and sardonic; its characters pointed out the ugliness of human nature.

Crommelynck was imbued with the spirit of these writers, past
and present; to their innovations he added his own. His theater may
be divided into two loosely knit categories: "The Theater of the
Unexpressed and the Tragic Farce" and "Toward the Boulevard."

VI · *The Theater of the Unexpressed and the Tragic Farce*

Like the Symbolist theater, the Theater of the Unexpressed
(which includes Crommelynck's *The Merchant of Regrets, The*

Sculptor of Masks, and *The Puerile Lovers*) sought to delineate an inner vision through suggestive imagery, nuanced sensations, and tenuous ideas. Unlike symbolist theater, however, the Theater of the Unexpressed did not have recourse to fairy tales or to myths; insofar as Crommelynck was concerned, its recourse was to the complexities and chaotic nature of human beings in everyday surroundings and situations. Psychology was an important factor in Crommelynck's Theater of the Unexpressed, but not the intellectual assessment and pathological situations that mark H. R. Lenormand's *Time is a Dream* or *The Eater of Dreams.* Rather, Crommelynck's method was to portray an underlying morbidity that leads to outbreaks of jealousy and even deaths, as in *The Sculptor of Masks.* In *The Puerile Lovers,* the inability to face the ravages of age leads to a pronounced schizophrenic condition that is never expressed as such but is subsumed, felt, or sensed by the characters. Crommelynck never includes dream sequences nor any curative agent. He dramatizes; he cuts open; he offers no remedies.

In the Theater of the Unexpressed the action usually takes place in some prosaic area, for example, a store in *The Sculptor of Masks,* a large living room in *The Puerile Lovers.* The plot is simple and devoid of complicated intrigues. All unnecessary chatter is banished. Words no longer reveal "soul states" as they did in the plays of Henry Bataille, Henri Bernstein, and Paul Hervieu. Such inner architecture had to be communicated through sighs, silences, or lyrical poetic passages.

The Theater of the Unexpressed is rooted in French classical tradition. Marivaux, a master in delving into the secrets of the heart, left much unsaid in *Game of Love and Chance,* in *The Second Love Surprise,* and in *Conquered Prejudice.* Although his plays are comic, neither laughter nor satire is essential. His characters are for the most part finely etched, in elegant, nuanced, and sometimes imperceptible lines. The love between the protagonists is hidden or repressed at the outset of the play and is allowed to blossom forth during the course of the acts. Marivaux wrote: "I observed all the different niches within the human heart where love could hide, where it is afraid to show itself; each of my comedies has as its goal to allow this love to emerge from its niche." A century earlier Molière also used "zones of silences" to exteriorize his characters' feelings.

The unexpressed in certain cases was far more powerful, he felt, than what was said. We know how annoyed Molière was by the pompous and dogmatic acting styles of the Comédie-Française tradition. Molière opted for a more attenuated method.

Other French forerunners of the Theater of the Unexpressed were Alfred de Vigny, Jules Renard and Jean-Jacques Bernard (Martine). De Vigny's character Kitty Bell in *Chatterton* expressed her love tacitly. A glance or a facial expression was sufficient to reveal her feelings. Renard's *Carrot Top* suggested his bent for cruelty via verbal jabs. His characters, far from loquatious, expressed their emotional involvement in a variety of verbal and nonverbal modulations. Maeterlinck wrote in *The Treasure of the Humble*: "as soon as we really have something to say we are obliged to remain silent." What fascinates is not what has been said but what is not yet verbalized.[17]

Chekhov was a master of the Theater of the Unexpressed. His characters in *The Cherry Orchard*, *The Three Sisters*, and *Uncle Vania* are resigned and remote in their thoughts and sentiments. They inhabit a strange world, an atmosphere imbued with melancholy based on a past that will never be revived. Their world, with its mysteries, includes moments of intense suspense and anguishing climaxes where conversation simply ceases.

In Crommelynck's *The Merchant of Regrets*, *The Sculptor of Masks*, and *The Puerile Lovers*, a whole inner world is focused upon but never really brought to light in the dialogue. Its impact on the viewer is marked through the imagery of sensuous poetry and the expert use of the mask, facial expressions, and versatile acting techniques. In *The Puerile Lovers* a dream quality is interjected into the stage happenings; vagueness of plot and character delineations propel viewers into a world where the fine demarcation lines between illusion and reality no longer exist—a world tinged with anguish and despair.

Elements of the Theater of the Unexpressed co-mingle with the spirit of the Tragic Farce in *The Magnificent Cuckold* and *Golden Tripe*. A violent and cruel yet humorous world is set before the viewer. In these plays Strindberg's influence—his pessimism as delineated in *The Father*, *Miss Julie*, and *The Dance of Death*—is strongly felt: man doomed to suffer forever—since Adam's fall for the crimes committed in some past existence. Although Crommelynck was an agnostic and did not believe in Strindberg's mystic lucubrations, Strindberg's nihilistic approach, his sharp repartees, and his excoriating types prevailing onstage did make their mark on Crommelynck.

Crommelynck's farces are not happy; indeed, they are touched with tragedy. In this respect they are in keeping with Ionesco's definition of the Tragic Farce: stage happenings of a violent, cruel, and absurd nature. For Ionesco, logic must be disrupted by the onslaught of improbable situations, eliciting nonsensical activity, unbelievable coincidences, and terminating in a crescendo of virulence. In *Victims of Duty*, Ionesco attempted to "drown the comic in the tragic; in *The Chairs*, the tragic in the comic . . . to oppose the comic with the tragic and to blend them into a new theatrical synthesis."[18] Crommelynck reveals a crumbling and disintegrating society whose values hamper man's evolution rather than encourage it. His world is peopled with grotesque characters making their plight known through horrendous outbursts. Absurd and unreal qualities enter into the frenetic antics of the protagonists; but, as in the delirious fantasy of Armand Salacrou's *Breaker of Plates*, humor clothes an underlying spirit of anguish and revulsion. Crommelynck's protagonists are jealous, frequently without reason; they live in a fantasy realm that makes reality painful to face. With the introduction of the absurd and the unreal into the stage happenings, anything can take place in the illogical world of the obsessed. Humor is experienced as an agent of destruction in *The Magnificent Cuckold* and is death-dealing in *Golden Tripe*.

Crommelynck's tragic-farce technique is phallus-oriented, originating in the ancient farces given in Megara in the fifth century B.C. It rests on the scabrous as well as on the intensity of the activities pursued on stage and the developments that arise from them. Comedy is more intellectual than farce. It is an outgrowth of character study, as demonstrated in *Tartuffe*, *The Miser*, and *The Misanthrope*. Farces, pointing up the humorous side of life, frequently use masks and stock characters from the *commedia dell'arte* repertoire. The characters speak with a particular accent, use stereotype expressions, and indulge in a variety of set behavior patterns. Molière included these techniques in *Scapin, the Trickster* as well as in some scenes of his other comedies; for example, in *The Imaginary Invalid* the physicians are reminiscent of the *commedia dell'arte*'s Dottore. More recently, Alfred Jarry's *King Ubu*, Guillaume Apollinaire's *The Breasts of Tiresias*, André Breton's and Philippe Soupault's *If You Please*, and Roger Vitrac's *The Mysteries of Love* belong to the farce category for the same reasons.

Crommelynck uses the slapstick routines of the farce in *Golden Tripe* and *The Magnificent Cuckold*, and his technique is precise, perhaps even mechanical at times. But the truculent dialogue and the buffoonlike natures of his characters provoke tragedy amid laughter. Henri Bergson was right, stating in his essay on "Laughter" that certain types of comedy are marked with "insensitivity," "automatism," and an "absence of feeling on the part of the observer."[19]

The ugliness of Crommelynck's characters is striking. They are like concretized monsters, scoundrels for the most part. The situations of marriage, inheritance, and law and order are unpleasant. Unlike Molière's usually light and bantering satire, Crommelynck's is heavy and negative. He seeks to destroy, not to rectify; to vilify and humiliate, not to reform and strengthen. Crommelynck's plots are mostly anarchic; he uses them to give free reign to his creatures. The madness of the situations he engenders and the amorality of the protagonists, who act on impulse, give rise to a nightmarish atmosphere—comparable to the surrealistic dramas of Vitrac (*The Mysteries of Love* and *Victor*). Obscure motivations reveal the complex and incomprehensible nature of man's psyche, and satire is used to provoke a dissociation between thought and expression.

Crommelynck's adaptation of Shakespeare's *Falstaff* (1954) was undertaken in this vein. A great admirer of the Elizabethan dramatist, Crommelynck decided to restore the original unity of *Falstaff*, which Shakespeare had divided into Parts I and II in *Henri IV*. To Crommelynck, Falstaff was the ultimate of comic figures, a kind of *miles gloriosus*: parasite and fool. Crommelynck was attracted to this "tun of flesh" who fed on deceptions, lies, and roguishness; who was as "gross as earth," ridiculous, a coward, and a blind lover. Samuel Johnson wrote:

Falstaff unimitated, unimitable Falstaff, how shall I describe thee? Though compound of sense and vice; of sense which may be admired but not esteemed, of vice which may be despised, but hardly detested.

VII   *Toward the Boulevard*

Carine, Hot and Cold, and *A Woman Whose Heart Is too Small* are lighter comedy and more in the boulevard tradition. This kind of comedy aims to please: its characterizations are more superficial, and its verse and power less virile. In his boulevard plays, Crommelynck avails himself of a central idea, or themes, and expands upon it. Sacha Guitry using a similar method successfully, expressed his belief: "What I call point of departure is frequently a minute idea . . . Once I constructed an entire scenario after having heard just a simple remark one person made to another." Guitry's play *Jealousy* was based on the old proverb, "It's a jealous husband that makes for an unfaithful wife." His plays were so popular that when speaking of him and his father, an actor, Lugné-Poë, said they were "a national treasure."

Jules Romains' influence is clearly discernible in *Hot and Cold,* in which the concept of unanimism is dramatized with felicity. The play deals with the collective's need for the myth and the individual's longing for a religious credo. Romains gave dramatic form to his unanimistic doctrine in *Donogoo Tonka*: a "famous" professor, a candidate for the French Institute, mentions a nonexistent town in South America, which then has to be founded so that he will not lose face. Romains used the same form in *Doctor Knock,* in which sickness becomes a collective phobia. His brand of humor is special, that of the *canulard*—dry, biting, and sardonic; so is Crommelynck's in *Hot and Cold* and in *A Woman Whose Heart Is too Small.* These plays reveal a blend of roguery with a dash of Voltarian piquancy. But Crommelynck's characters are anthropophagous in addition to their wit. They symbolically eat each other up during the course of the events.

Crommelynck's theater ridicules, destroys, inflates, and deflates amid a series of frequently incongruous situations. His plays are "as disorderly as his life," said Roger Blin; his protagonists as "irascible" as he—bitter, jealous, and tormented.[20] Crommelynck clothes his beings in garbs of fun and frolic, but in reality they emerge as vehicles expressing his own sharp commentary on human nature. The skirmishes and reversals of fortune that oscillate throughout each of Crommelynck's plays underscore the crudeness and uncouth nature of his beings: their chicanery, knavery, lust, and desire for evil. There are no heroes in Crommelynck's plays; his characters represent a carnival of human folly in which man's vanity, egotism, and cruelty are brought forth in all of their disquieting grandeur.

CHAPTER 2

The Sculptor of Masks:
The Transposition of Art (1911)

"**T**RAGICALLY painted, admirably sculpted, of an original and violent beauty," *The Sculptor of Masks* "gives access to the red and tenebrous palace of the most anguishing of human passions,"[1] wrote Emile Verhaeren. Crommelynck's three-act prose play is a powerful drama of repressed passions, unavowed jealousies, and psychological multilations.[2] It was successfully performed in Paris at the Théâtre du Gymnase in 1911.

The Sculptor of Masks has been labeled Impress Theater or more exactly *Theater of the Unexpressed*. Feelings and emotions are revealed through gesture, protracted silences, an interplay of chiaroscuro, and through provocative sound effects. Decor and sets are realistic, like a transposition of art, but emotions are hidden, veiled, and mysterious, and seem to thrive in an insalubrious inner climate. Of import to Crommelynck is what is sensed and fleeting. Such undercurrents of emotions are transmitted indirectly through glances, sighs, and subtle cries, expressing a panoply of feelings that range from remorse to hatred. The protagonists' soul states are concretized in their facial expressions; then eternalized in the variety of masks peopling the stage. According to Henri de Régnier, the Theater of the Unexpressed consists in the "greatest suppression possible of verbal developments." Drama must be "guessed rather than explicated"; emotions "must be perceived and felt in the milieu in which they emerge through minute details which suggest (and) which render them present without explaining them." Sentiments must be allowed "to become manifest involuntarily through the activities implicit in the routine of life and not isolated from it; they

31

must be interwoven and blended into the events and sensations—
thus creating a unit."[3]

I *The Plot*

The Sculptor of Masks takes place in Pascal's store studio in the
ancient Spanish-Flemish town of Bruges. Pascal is an artist-poet,
the creator of "grotesque, terrible, and charming" masks. The
background of Bruges—its church steeples, factories, Béguinage
tower, canal, and forest areas—is visible on stage. City noises are
audible: the anvil with its "regular hammer beat"; the town clock,
which determines the rhythmic movement of the stage happenings;
children at play, the chirping of birds, the cries of the merchants
selling their wares. A different atmosphere prevails inside the store.
Madeleine is crying. Louison, her sister and Pascal's wife, cannot
understand the reason for her despair. Madeleine stops weeping
suddenly. The two sisters begin to talk as they paint the wooden
masks that hang about the shop. The audience slowly becomes
aware that Pascal is in love with Madeleine, and though her passion
is controlled, she loves him too. The din of rambunctious children at
play is heard. Like a pack of wild animals, they approach the store to
mock and taunt the two sisters. Their ferocious escapades mirror the
antagonism the staid city folk bear toward the artist and all he represents. The city's inhabitants also make their sentiments known toward Pascal and his family. The carpenter stops for a chat, as do the
bird catcher, the doctor, and some merchants. Each gazes at the
masks and reacts either pityingly, angrily, or entranced, to the deformed or beautiful features these wooden faces symbolize. Pascal,
entering the store, tells the visitors of the veiled meanings of these
effigies: "legends are hidden within the masks." They represent a
lifetime of activity, feeling, pain, and joy. When the doctor stops in
front of the store, Pascal plays the clown and refuses him entrance.
"The carnival is here," Pascal cries out, implying that sickness and
death must be sought elsewhere. Louison leaves on an errand.
Alone with Madeleine, Pascal, in a moment of passion, embraces
her brutally. She fights to free herself. When Louison returns, she
senses Pascal's attraction for Madeleine and collapses.

Louison has become ill and the doctor and her sister take care of her. Her heart has been weakened and she cannot last much longer. Louison knows she is dying and longs for that moment of oblivion. Never once does she reveal her feelings of despair and the pain that corrodes her being. Pascal grows increasingly impatient with his wife. He cannot bear her saintly ways, her passivity, her suffering, and her spirit of self-sacrifice. He seeks life in the raw: joy, activity, chaos, argumentation, conflict. This is the food from which his creative factor is kindled.

The city is now decorated with colored lanterns, visible in the distance. It is Mardi Gras time. Joy and festivity permeate the air outside the shop. The villagers dance, sing, and carry on in wild disarray, dissimulating their anger toward the unfaithful Pascal and their rejection of the artist in society. As they enjoy the fanfare of abandon, their laughter grows louder, their screams less contained. In sharp contrast, the events within the store grow more lugubrious. Louison is about to die. The merrymakers, some of whom are disguised as hangmen, enter the store. "A good farce," one says to the other, thus momentarily dispelling the macabre atmosphere. Pandemonium increases. Pascal enters and spectators crowd his store. Each of the masks has been donned by an actor who weaves and pivots his way around the stage. Pascal looks at these floating emanations, these disembodied personalities, and is dazed. Silence descends. The door to the next room opens and Madeleine announces her sister's death. Pascal will not believe it. She is out dancing, he claims. "She will dance all night." Raucous and tumultuous yells fill the air and fanfare permeates the stage. Death has descended amidst peels of laughter. The priest gives the last rites. The carnival atmosphere with its spirit of exhilaration and frenetic activity pursues its bawdy course.

II *Characterizations*

Besides being Theater of the Unexpressed, *The Sculptor of Masks* is also a psychological drama. The protagonists (Louison, Madeleine and Pascal) are beings of flesh and blood with all the lusts, fears, and desires they can have. Theirs is a triumvirate of love, guilt, and remorse. These emotions are lived inwardly for the most part and expressed outwardly in the artist's creative masks. Clothed in an atmosphere of mystery and poetic beauty, *The Sculptor of Masks* is reminiscent of the symbolical dramas, *The Blind* and *The Intruder*, by Maeterlinck.

Louison represents the celestial martyr type. She is an immaculate being who prefers to suffer rather than to hurt others; to die rather than to release her torment. She is what Balzac termed the *ange-femme*, the self-abnegating woman, the sacrificing mother, the ultrasensitive being that represents Christian values. Verhaeren called her "anguish personified."[4]

Early in the play Louison discovers she is unloved. "Taciturn and resigned," Henri de Régnier wrote, "she suffers secretly." Her pain, however, is not hers alone. She exhudes pathos and fills the atmosphere with gloom. Her agony is experienced by her husband, who lives in her dimension as well as in his own.[5] Pascal cannot stand the spirit of resignation and passivity she symbolizes. Irritated by her mutism, he provokes her, wanting her to express her torment, preferring an attack on her part. Louison, however, is incapable of overt acts, verbal or otherwise. As his annoyance grows more blatant, his rejection of her spiritually oriented world becomes more open. Around her he intimates unfolds a repressive domain. She imposes her ideations upon the household, stifling all that comes within her reach. Her soft, sweet, and angelic ways render the atmosphere unlivable.

Louison is simple in all ways. Her outlook and demeanor never vary; her love for Pascal is complete (as she understands it) and intense. He was her god from the moment she first met him and would always remain so. She takes pleasure in recounting their first walk together near the lake. She describes the winds and the clouds in their elusive and eternal flux, thus using nature metaphorically for her husband's alternating moods.

> And toward the evening the sky became lacerated
> and he saw clouds of all colors fall slowly behind
> the city . . . (p. 243)

The image thus delineated is almost premonitory. It depicts semiotically the pain Louison will suffer; the disenchantment of all of her spiritual values; the end of her world conceived as purity. Centered upon her husband, Louison spends her time adoring him; but after she has caught him kneeling in front of her sister, she wants to die. Never once does she speak a word of reproach and simulates joy and unconcern. However, when alone with her sister, she explodes into tears. Mortally wounded by Pascal's love for Madeleine, her agony is poignantly translated in her facial expressions.

Pascal the artist-creator, visceral and strong, represents the earth principle and is therefore subject to alternating passions, views, and attitudes. He loves life and needs to confront real human beings. He is Dionysian in that he feels a sense of renewal after expressing himself, as evinced when he passionately grabbed Madeleine. His feelings toward Louison grow more and more ambivalent until he finally hates her. He despises this angel who is incapable of penetrating his world based on lust, activity, and conflict. His vitality, brutality, impulsiveness are rejected by the introverted and sacrosanct Louison.

Madeleine is a guilt-ridden human being. She loves her sister and she would never hurt her. Madeleine, unlike Louison, is beautiful. She resembles the Mary Magdalene in the Bible. She cries throughout the early part of the drama—understanding the pain she is causing her sister. Although she controls herself and her passion, her feelings cannot be contained. Her love for Pascal will not be abated. She represents "life" and excitement. These personality traits are revealed in her obvious use of the verb "to live" throughout the drama. She seeks to flee the repressive and tenebrous atmosphere created by her self-sacrificing sister, but is not strong enough to break the ties. She longs, as does Pascal, for the sun-drenched climes, where freedom and fun seem unlimited. Madeleine lives an inner drama, controlled on the outside but flamboyant in those hidden realms of her psyche.

Each of the protagonists unwittingly destroys the object of his or her love. Louison needs the realm of absolute perfection in which to thrive. Such a world is anathema to the artist; it is arid, infertile territory. His masks, molded from his very flesh, are born from his sensations and visions that must be nourished and fertilized by both inner and outer sources. His imagination transmutes the impalpable into concrete objects. Inspiration for Pascal emerges from the impact of eidetic images, those that haunt and taunt his unconscious. His masks contain a lifetime of feeling. He maintains: "I will write legends behind these masks" (p. 250). Pascal is forever burgeoning with ideas and excitement. Young, vital, optimistic, his creativity at the outset of the play knows no bounds. Flooded with inspiration, he ferrets out all that lives within him. He sees an artistic creation in the hushed climate of Louison's dark inner world and in Madeleine's captivating hilarity. He magnifies what is infinitesimal; externalizes the fleeting. Pascal's masks take on stature as the play progresses and become protagonists in themselves, representing the bruised or blessed faces of humanity.

It is not only the human world that acts as a source of creativity for Pascal; nature also arouses him tacitly. When alone in the woods, he feels himself part of the tree, experiences the odor of resin throughout his body, the unctuousness of the sap as it flows through the fibers of his being. He breathes in the aroma of the grass and the flower blossoms. These sensations and feelings he transmutes into his masks. Pascal uses the world as a whole to survive—to create. He cannot experience only part of it, spirit alone, which Louison represents.

During his moments of intense creativity, Pascal feels driven to leave his shop and its stifling atmosphere. He needs to be unconstrained—to confront tumult and excitement offered him by a world made up of infinite possibilities and wondrous things and people. During these febrile moments he believes himself capable of "curing all evils," penetrating all objects, and elevating man to understand the nobler and more beautiful things in life. He refuses to let his emotions starve to death and be treated like a pariah. He simply cannot live conventionally and cannot fulfill the bourgeois code of ethics. The townspeople believe that each individual should serve a useful purpose and should act for society as a whole. "What a strange trade!" says the doctor, when looking at Pascal's masks (p. 272). He suggests that Pascal is wasting his time and energy.

Pascal is rejected by the townspeople for yet another reason, his "unfaithfulness" to his wife. The deception he practises counters their social, religious, and moral conventions. Scorned by Pascal, they stand for subservience, hypocrisy, prententiousness, and avariciousness. His hostility toward them is symbolized in each of his masks, mirror images of those he denigrates.

Collective anger is expressed theatrically by the stone-throwing children. Each time projectiles are thrust and windows in Pascal's store are shattered, a high point in society's rancor against the artist is marked. Brute force is used to crush a personality and its creative principle. Such activities are a sad commentary by Crommelynck on man, with his wars and conflagrations, his hatreds and jealousies. The playwright also darts his arrows on the inhabitants of such Flemish cities as Ostend, Bruges, Ghent with their sumptuous city halls, palacial homes, impressive church spires. Victims of pretentiousness, of fetiches, the people featured in *The Sculptor of Masks* present a bold front based on piety and peace when in reality they indulge in the most illicit of existences.

The artist, as personified by Pascal, must not be evaluated as an ordinary individual. He transcends the conventional man and must be nourished by life in all its variety. Louison, therefore, cannot possibly satisfy him since she represents only passivity and self-sacrifice, mutism and introspection. His creative faculties demand aggressive forces, those possessed by Madeleine. It is upon constantly shifting soil and substance that he thrives. His needs alter with each of his creations. Because he is sensitive, he understands the pain he inflicts on others: "I am a person filled with sadness and folly" (p. 262). Each time he feels submerged by guilt, he fights for freedom within himself. Louison's inward goodness cuts off his growth; she uproots those succulent and fertile elements within him. A constant reminder of his egotism, her death wish symbolizes his unconscious murderous intent. The silence in the shop whenever Louison is around makes Pascal realize: "I am a prisoner of my nerves as a spider is prisoner of its web; it is painful" (p. 269).

The artist who deals with universals must frequently reject conventions and renounce halfhearted situations. However, Pascal cannot escape his upbringing, nor his guilt and sorrow at the destruction he has wrought. As the smell of death encroaches, the city—a mass hysteria—closes in upon Pascal's world. Once again children cast stones at his shop, a transposition of the lapidation attempt on the adulterous woman (John 8:7). Pascal's ire is aroused at the callousness of the outside world. He wants revenge. Ardent in his passions, he leaves his shop, intent upon giving the world a trouncing. He refuses to allow the destruction of his masks. Pascal arms for battle but moments later returns with his clothes torn and his hair disheveled. Louison is startled by such overt mob anger. The razor-sharp glass from the shattered windows is strewn about the shop and symbolizes the pain she feels. "You would be aghast! aghast, I tell you if you could understand my pain!" (p. 283) she murmurs.

Pascal's mood has altered. Intoxicated with life once again, he looks upon the antics perpetrated by the young and old as a kind of comedy, a game, a masquerade. He believes that agitation and hostility of others strengthen one. Conflict must create chaos within the artist in order to bring forth the new. Art is an aggressive act; each fresh image and every new value must be extracted from the flesh. The world thrives on struggle and battle, excitement and novelty. Love, too, is nourished on jealousy and anger. Once love has kindled these titanic forces within man, it cannot be considered sacrosanct anymore—to be worshipped like a precious but sterile object. Nor is love beautiful: "If someone told you that love is beautiful and smiling, like a doll, he lied" (p. 289).

Pascal taunts and insults Louison, repudiating her values. He acts out his aggressions and demands her anger in return: "I want to hear you cry, you cry at least once" (p. 289). It is human, not divine, nature that Pascal seeks in his companion for life; not the consoling and (s)mothering martyr type. Emotions of guilt aroused within him when he observes her white skin and her trembling lips cause him to confess his love for her. But then his rancor builds up again: "I'll go crazy! . . . The need to lie is in my veins, in my mind, in the marrow of my bones! . . . My blood poisons me" (p. 293). During his turmoil, Pascal confesses his hatred for Louison to Madeleine: "I want to destroy her, to pounce on her—with my two hands clutched tightly around her neck! I long for her death" (p. 293). Whereas Louison's weakness and passivity disgust him, Madeleine's zest for life, lust, and excitement attract him: "When you used to look at me, I felt my heart ripen like a fruit" (p. 295).

Act III is an apotheosis. Life and death are viewed together in the celebration of the carnival. In Roman Catholic countries just before Lent, varied parades, masquerades, and pageants were enacted. The origin of this festive period was pre-Christian and symbolized the joys connected with fertility rites and with the coming of spring and vegetation. In Egypt such wild merrymaking was associated with Osiris' resurrection; in Greece, with Dionysus' rejuvenation. Frequently the Greeks constructed floats dedicated to Dionysus, a joyful and ribald god. In Roman periods, disorder and wantonness marked the Bacchanalian, Saturnalian, and Lupercalian festivities. Because the Catholic Church was powerless in eradicating this need for joy and rebirth, the Church accepted the feasts as part of its ritual. In medieval periods the season for renewal was manifested in celebrations such as the Feast of Fools, which included a mock mass and a blasphemous impersonation of church officials, as in the bawdy rituals of the Feast of the Ass.

Crommelynck interwove this joyful atmosphere with the solemnity of death, blending the sacred and the profane. Man was allowed to indulge his passions before the fasting of Lent. This juxtaposition of joy and pathos is manifested by the revelers invading Pascal's store. The contrast between the carousing city folk—the flashy colored lights, garlands, stained-glass windows, musicmakers—and the pain and anguish brought by Louison's death is striking. Pascal's heart is filled with love and desire as he looks out at the world. Inside his shop, the lugubrious, regressive, and guilt-ridden atmosphere still exists. Pascal refuses to feel any pain. He rejects his remorse that is about to strangle him: "I do not want to be vanquished, do you understand?" (p. 300) And to Madeleine, moments later, he bewails that Louison never understood him and never experienced his passion. As Louison's death approaches, Pascal describes his tortured feelings:

I took her face into my hands, and then—then—I was terrorized. Her face was so marked with pain that I thought its contours would remain imprinted upon my flesh, like the face of Jesus on Saint Veronica's clothing. (p. 301)

Pascal reproaches himself for his wife's dismal fate. Meanwhile, gruesome and distorted masked skeletons make their way into his shop. Clothed in sheets and frightening costumes, these fantasms hover about and terrify the artist-poet. They represent the guilt and fear that will forever harass him. These supernatural and hideous creatures represent sickness and madness. As they prance about the stage, vacantly eying Pascal, their ghastly rictus is imprinted on his mind. These gargoylelike beings wearing Pascal's masks rise power- fully before him, taunting and torturing him. Under the sway of such excoriating kinetic sculptures, Pascal edges back in an attempt to reach safety. His eyes fix upon the next room where Louison lies. A cry of pain is heard amid the din of merrymaking. Terrified, Madeleine clutches Pascal and he says: "Let's run away. Let's not wait any longer; if we do, we'll vomit on ourselves." Madeleine agrees. As another sharp cry is heard, she stands as if paralyzed. Pascal takes her in his arms and confesses that Louison's agony never leaves him, that he has sculpted her pain into all of his masks. He points to a series of tragic masks, which suddenly come to life. Pascal fails to stop them. The masks move around the proscenium as in a funeral procession. When Pascal sees these mobile effigies of his wife, he collapses and Madeleine runs out.

Verhaeren wrote the following:

The drama was like a mad tornado spend itself out in front of the protagonists—going from one plane to the other, ploying the trees, uproot- ing the grass, knocking over the thatched houses, lacerating the horizon. The last gradation was admirably obtained. The conclusion was logical and sinister. All the masks Pascal had sculpted had acquired a morally terrifying significance. And death intruded finally in the midst of the laughter of the carnival and the prayers of the priest tore at the heart, like tragic patches. It was superb and very simple.[6]

III *Theater as a Transposition of Art*

The Sculptor of Masks is much more than a psychological drama; it is a *transposition of art*. Baudelaire, Gautier, Flaubert, and Huysmans used this art form in poetry, the short story, and the novel. Maeterlinck modeled his narrative *The Massacre of the Inno- cents* after Brueghel's painting with the same name. Crommelynck was one of the first to use the transposition-of-art form for theatrical purposes, thus paving the way for Apollinaire (*The Breasts of Tiresias*), Cocteau (*The Wedding on the Eiffel Tower*), Claudel (*The Satin Slipper*), and more recently for Robert Wilson (*Deafman Glance*) Wilson's huge mobile collages feature puppets, masked figures, and polymorphous objects inspired by the works of Magritte, Ernst, Rousseau, Van Dongen and others.

In *The Sculptor of Masks*, Crommelynck appears to have been inspired by the works of James Ensor, the Flemish artist whom he befriended in 1908. The powerful canvases *The Woman in Distress* and *The Entry of Christ into Brussels* (1888) impressed Crommelynck.[7] His eye for space and color, for architectural planes, his feeling for mood and tone, and his metaphysical probings enabled him to capture and replicate certain features inherent in Ensor's hallucinatory visions. Crommelynck's use of the mask in *The Sculptor of Masks* also resembles Ensor's notions concerning this primitive "religious" device. Both men used the mask to scorn the so-called pillars of society with their sententious ideas and their hypocritical ways. They also used it as a means of concretizing man's distorted inner world, his yearning for beauty and his engulfment in putrefaction.

In keeping with the Flemish atmosphere in Ensor's paintings, Crommelynck's play exudes realistic and mystical plenitude. It is replete with religious primitivism. A world is created in which malevolent and titanic ogres and good-willed fairies exist, a domain of saintliness and eroticism. Viewers of *The Sculptor of Masks* will be initiated into the mysteries of Flemish life, an arcane world in which shadows and demons hover about in harmony and cacophony.

The Sculptor of Masks, like Ensor's canvases, is situated outside of time and space. In this elusive and limitless atmosphere, the macrocosm is concretized by the busy street scene; the hustle and bustle of a town at play with its rambunctious and insidious forces, its madness and fascination. The microcosm is exemplified by Pascal's shop: a silent, lugubrious, and sanctified world in which each individual attempts to deal with his own terrors in his own way.

The strange lighting effects in *The Sculptor of Masks*, as well as in Ensor's canvases, not only create a dialectic between the visible and the invisible worlds, but also inject eerie and harsh tonalities on the events being enacted onstage. Act I and Act II are inundated with lights that fall on the masks in sheets, waves, and in a series of shadowy reverberations. In Act III these same flamelike intrusions take on a magical quality, as the store, now obscurely lit, contrasts with the festivities and kaleidoscopic effects in the street during carnival time. Silence and mystery as contrasted with excitement and motility are evoked by the lights, used as tangible instruments for the creation of atmosphere.

Man's baffling nature and his explosive torment are further delineated by the events depicted outside the shop. There, the world is forever imposing itself upon the more slowly paced happenings within the shop. The working society views the intimate details of marital conflicts, a replica of their own individual existences. The punctuated intrusion of the outer realm (the city) upon the inner world (the shop) creates a dichotomy in the rhythms and alternating emotions, pointing up the abrasive and tender qualities implicit within man.

Pascal's store is reminiscent of Ensor's attic studio in Ostend where the painter spent many years. Located above his parents' souvenir shop, it was decorated with shells, puppets, parrots, carnival masks, dolls, marionettes, beads, artificial flowers and fabrics of all kinds. The diversified objects inspired his creative faculties. In *Intrigue* (1890), Ensor depicts the haunting and bizarre color effects of grotesquely masked faces, delineating "elusive passions . . . bathed in the captivating and poisonous light of Ensorian ambiguity."[8] The multiplicity of emotions, the mazelike quality so characteristic of Ensor's works probably inspired Crommelynck to create his grotesque and hallucinatory beings with their equivocal and tantalizing natures.

Both Crommelynck and Ensor understood the proximity between gravity and buffoonery, tragedy and comedy, laughter and tears. For them, life touched on all of these polarities. The masks depicted by Ensor in the painting *Old Woman with Masks* (1889) are ones of utter disillusionment with a "sickly and vacant stare."[9] In *The Despair of Pierrot*, the Christlike Pierrot surrounds himself with the coarsest and basest members of humanity, such as moneylenders and procuresses, all of whom wear masks to deceive the rest of mankind.

For both the dramatist and the painter, love was not merely a question of self-sacrifice, saintliness, or turning the other cheek, as the Christian dictum supposes, but rather, love was a life-force in which serenity and anger, guilt and self-satisfaction, spirituality and sexuality, as well as action, joy, authenticity, and conflict cohabit. For Crommelynck and Ensor, love was a lusty, vital emotion that had to be experienced fully if life was to be "really" lived. Laughter in *The Sculptor of Masks* is never vulgar, neither is lust. Adultery, depicted in grim tones and with macabre humor, jolts the viewers out of their lethargy and is considered a necessary force in life.

The mask for Crommelynck and for Ensor held specific significance. "I have joyously shut myself up in the solitary domain where the mask holds sway, wholly made up of violence, light, and brilliance," wrote Ensor. The mask represented a freshness of expression; an intensity of tone, and a sumptuous background for emotions, "unplanned movements, exquisite turbulence."[10] The mask is an instrument capable of exaggerating the grotesque, the whimsical, the freaks of nature, the grimaces, and the irascible expressions. Like Pierrot, Pascal enters the world of the misunderstood. A kind of pariah, he tries to lead and inspire the mob with his fresh ideas of life and to teach the masses about the creative factor. The artist, depicted by Crommelynck, tries to dominate his world but is stifled instead and suffers the fate of many talented people.

For both Crommelynck and Ensor the mask expresses an inner dimension, facets of the personality that are scattered about in cubistic disarray. The masks aligned in Pascal's shop are reminiscent of the medieval "Dances of Death": from the pope to the lowest peasant all were equal in death. Such "Dances of Death," led by the skeleton in merry escapades, were depicted in medieval times on walls of churchyards and cemeteries, in drawings by Holbein, in a ballad by Goethe, and in music by Saint-Saëns and Liszt. For Crommelynck, this dance did not have the leveling effect implicit in the fourteenth century. He looked upon this ancient dance as a morbid rephrasing of fear, guilt, terror, and remorse that captured and enslaved those who allowed themselves to be dominated by the philosophy of the Church. Pascal, though he lived with negativism, a self-sacrificing wife, and her sister who loved him, rejected the sanctification of self-abnegation and the overevaluated notions of pain and torture. He kindled within him a Nietzschean zest for life and excitement. But pain and remorse did haunt him. When these emotions held sway, his masks took on the dimensions of gargoyles, grimacing forces with demoniacal overtones imprisoning within their fearsome expressions monstrous and excoriating attitudes.

Neither Crommelynck nor Ensor allowed themselves to be imprisoned by the gruesome aspects of existence, but combined these morbid qualitites with the carnival. In his painting *Carnival on the Beach*, Ensor captures the dichotomy within man: his sado-masochism and his joy and lust for life. Crommelynck also depicts these feelings within Pascal and the two sisters, each representing distinct polarities. During carnival time, Crommelynck and Ensor must have observed the variety of masks used to dispel fear and encourage merrymaking. The anguished appearance in *The Sculptor of Masks* of these disembodied heads bobbing up and down in the crowd in Act III, or static in Acts I and II, gave the impression of formidable beings and nonbeings. Fright and alienation ensued. The tinsel and artificiality of the carnival spirit made deep impressions on the protagonists and audience. In Act III, for example, fantastic forms peered into the stage areas. Like allegorical figures representing vice, passion, and anger, some of these forms, clothed in white sheets, seemed to float about in subsist designs, teasing and deriding Pascal for his lechery. Sounds of all types invaded the stage, faint rustles, tolling of bells, and cackling sounds. The strangeness of man's imaginings was conveyed by Crommelynck sensorially with body signals, visually with the masks; spacially by the exits and entrances of fantasms.

Perhaps the most moving depiction of all was the macabre nature of death's entrance into man's world. The deliberate and tragic crescendo of emotions as Louison's demise approached and as Pascal became increasingly overcome by his guilt was depicted by misshapen and writhing forms. Death manifests itself deliberately and tragically as well as with the humor of a Beckett and a Genet in such plays as *Endgame* or *The Blacks*. Crommelynck's derisive laughter makes a mockery of Louison's death. Pascal's disbelief when presented with the facts is based on his disenchantment with human nature, his powerlessness before life, and the absurdity of man's condition. Like Ensor's creatures, so Crommelynck's are distorted by sorrow. They quiver and turn as they try to wriggle away from man's unalterable finitude.

As a theatrical device the masks serve to both hide and reveal, their very ambiguity increasing the tensions between the visible and invisible worlds of illusion and reality. Since earliest times, masks have been used in religious ceremonies and represent unreal aspects of gods, goddesses, demons, and animal forces. The mask in Crommelynck's drama is an expression of the mutable self that is forever being modified by the individual during the course of his worldly existence and by the artist as he creates his work. The mask hides or protects his inner nature, a mystery to others—unreal, divine, and even demoniacal. As in the Japanese No drama, the mask separates the inchoate from the formed, the unconscious from the conscious. In ancient Egypt, masks were used to represent death; funerary masks were fixed on mummies to bind their erring souls. In *The Sculptor of Masks,* from the beginning of the drama, the mask became the harbinger of death, the semiotic spokesman for psychological and physical disease.

Crommelynck views the mask as representing the inexpressible, the tenuous, the preformal state of man before destiny has taken hold—the world of contingency. It is also an instrument of possession, a paradigm of the poet's hallucinatory realm. It underscores the supernatural in nature and man's fantasms. Crommelynck's use of the mask somewhat resembles that of O'Neill, as expressed in O'Neill's essay "Memoranda on Masks."

. . . masks will be discovered eventually to be the freest solution of the modern dramatist's problem as to how—with the greatest possible dramatic clarity and economy of means—he can express those profound hidden conflicts of the mind which the probings of psychology continue to disclose to us. He must find some method to present this inner drama in his work, or confess himself incapable of portraying one of the most characteristic preoccupations and uniquely significant, spiritual impulses of his time.[11]

The mask vivifies the artist's tendencies toward alienation, his attitude toward unfamiliar sites and strange visions that emerge in swift succession from his imaginary realm. In Pascal's shop, each of the masks represents an outward aspect of the human personality, capable upon contact with another of evoking social relationships or of arousing deep-seated feelings of indignation, dissatisfaction, yearning and sensuality.

The contemporary dramatist Fernando Arrabal employed masks and plaster effigies of beautiful women in *The Grand Ceremonial* to depict erotic rituals and perverse activities. In *The Blacks*, Jean Genet used the mask to build up a series of explosive emotions within the spectators, thus destroying their complacency, instead instilling fear, guilt, panic, confusion, and shattering empathy. Masks and larger-than-life-size puppets are the central figures in Peter Schumann's Bread and Puppet Theater. They concretize a weird inner life and magnify emotions.

The Sculptor of Masks is not meant to express emotion *per se*, as in what Brecht calls "culinary" theater, plays to be eaten, digested, and dismissed as illusion. These masks are intended instead to become ingrained in the flesh of the viewer as they do in the psyche of the protagonist—to nourish future thought and meditation. Masks may be looked upon as a kind of "montage," a key to further experiences, a catalyst. These wooden replicas of man's faces arouse visceral rapports between the inanimate and animate worlds, thus expanding man's frame of reference and, hopefully, bringing fresh attitudes into existence.

The mask is *phenomenon* in Heideggerian terms: that which reveals itself, which allows itself to be seen and to exist. Its form enables it to take part in the environment in which it has been placed. It has *Dasein* in Crommelynck's play. Thus it stirs relationships and participates in both individual and collective concerns. The mask shares in the communal world. It creates *Angst* and diminishes it as well. For Crommelynck, Ensor, and Brecht, the mask is not intended to capture or hold illusions. It must not be looked upon as a hypnotic device to mesmerize viewers. On the contrary, Crommelynck, the symbolist-expressionist, considers it a representative of the poet's yearnings, anxieties, feelings of remorse, guilt, and ugliness. Masks act as a buffer against the harshness and indifference of an absurd world; a device enabling Crommelynck's protagonists to deceive those in whom they cannot place their trust.

Viewing *The Sculptor of Masks* or an Ensor canvas, audiences are exposed to man's callous nature, his loves and hates. The artist is mocked, torn, crucified by those who claim to love him. Such love is egotistical and destructive to both self and the world. Were love truly altruistic, it would have been aware of the needs of the artist-creator, or the prophet, the complexities of such creative people. For all of her so-called saintliness, Louison attempted to dominate her husband, to mold him into her own pattern, to fit this vastly ebullient force into the constricting morality and conventional norms for which she stood. At best her love can be called self-indulgent.

The Sculptor of Masks is a study in the steady and ineluctable march of destruction. The poignancy of the drama, its superb rhythmic episodes, the harrowing gradations of its characterizations, are manipulated with expertise through the mask. It is no wonder that Albert Mocketl called it "paroxystic" theater, that Gabriel Marcel pointed to its "authenticity,"[12] and that Verhaeren commented on the "electrifying" nature of its language and the "novelty and splendor" of its imagery.

CHAPTER 3

The Magnificent Cuckold:
A Phallic Ritual (1920)

THE performance of *The Magnificent Cuckold* on December 18, 1920 at the Théâtre de l'Oeuvre, under the direction of Lugné-Poë, made theatrical history. Its success was accredited to the truculence and verve of its dialogue, the theme of jealousy transformed into a perversion, and Lugné-Poë's unforgettable interpretation of the protagonist.

The Magnificent Cuckold may be looked upon as a twentieth-century reenactment of the Greek comus: a joyful procession dramatized by the Megarians and Dorians in honor of Dionysus. These fun-filled celebrations, in which an effigy of the phallus was carried about in merriment and veneration, were expressions of the ecstasy experienced by the participants during their seasonal fertility rites. Like the Greek comus, the central image is the phallus. Although the phallus is not actually carried by the actors in Crommelynck's ribald farce, it is borne, symbolically within the psyche. Unlike in the Dionysian festival, Crommelynck's phallus neither elicits rapture, nor delight, nor hope as experienced so potently by the ancient celebrants. On the contrary, as conceived in *The Magnificent Cuckold,* the phallus arouses anger and jealousy, and terminates with the destruction of a personality.

I   *The Plot*

The play opens with the beautiful young Stella standing in front of her home, a converted windmill. Singing to the birds and flowers, she awaits the return of her poet-husband Bruno. A cowherd approaches stealthily. He begins making advances and tries to carry

48

her off. Stella's nurse rushes out of the house and helps her mistress fight off the intruder. Moments after the cowherd has left, the village count arrives and attempts, to no avail, to win her affections. Stella loves Bruno and remains faithful to him. Her husband returns with Petrus, Stella's handsome young captain cousin. Bruno begins a rapturous poetical tirade about his wife's physical and spiritual beauty; he goes into panegyrics about her birthmark in a very special place. Having apprised everyone of Stella's "divine" beauty, Bruno wants to prove the veracity of his remarks and asks Stella to raise her skirts, unbutton her blouse, and show off her breasts to Petrus. Utterly abashed by such a request, she nevertheless acquieses, to please her husband. Bruno notices a flicker of passion in Petrus's eye—a perfectly normal reaction to such feminine pulchritude. Bruno gets into an uncontrollable temper and strikes Petrus. From this moment on, jealousy erodes his being and he asks his best friend, Estrugo, the village scribe, to confirm Stella's fidelity. Before a reply is forthcoming, Bruno concludes in the negative.

In Act II Bruno accuses Stella of telling monstrous lies and of having a secret lover. He contrives a variety of traps to catch her and is, as is to be expected, unsuccessful every time. His uncertainty drives him to desperate measures. He asks Petrus to have sexual relations with Stella. Bruno believes the opposite of what he sees and what he is told. He reasons that if he finds her with a lover or two, he will believe the opposite of what he observes and she would be able to prove her innocence. Petrus refuses Bruno's request; but Stella begs him to yield. Finally, Petrus states: "Be cuckold he who wants to be" (p. 76). Bruno asks Estrugo to look through the keyhole and report what occurs between Petrus and Stella. Estrugo follows orders. In keeping with his reverse-reality reasoning, Bruno is now convinced of his wife's innocence. She is really untarnished. But is she?

In Act III Bruno attempts to further prove Stella's fidelity. He forces her to give herself to many young men. Although he sees them pawing and petting her in public, Bruno is still convinced he is not a cuckold. Would she indulge so openly in her sexual activities, he questions, had they really taken place? He rationalizes that she could not. Bruno simply asks them to be more tender toward her:

"One must conserve her in her entirety in order to share her" (p. 87). Estrugo cannot believe that Bruno allows this situation to persist. "Don't believe your eyes," Bruno replies (p. 89). The burgomaster and townswomen arrive demanding that this scandalous activity cease. Tired of trying to prove her love to her husband, Stella informs him that she is leaving him for the cowherd whom she kisses on the mouth in front of her disbelieving husband. Bruno's fantasy has become reality, his merry insanity leads him to believe that his wife's departure is but another huge joke, and he bursts into guffaws.

II *Phallic Mirth and Its Pathological Overtones*

Crommelynck's humor does not evoke belly laughter. It is sardonic, ridiculing, and destructive, closely akin to those spasmodic reactions Baudelaire labeled "laughter" and which he defined as a "perpetual explosion of his (the author's) anger and suffering."[1] The phallus, the *raison d'être* of *The Magnificent Cuckold*, enables Crommelynck to distill his strange concoction: to create a Bruno who believes only the reverse of reality. The phallus is the agent used by the dramatist to reveal Bruno's increased mental aberration. It is the *sine qua non* of his world: the single ingredient in his total existence. Unlike Molière's misanthropic Alceste, or his Barbouillé, or his Arnolphe of *The School for Wives*, wherein the protagonists had good reason to indulge their bitterness when their suspicions were founded in fact, Bruno's fantasies are expressions of his childish, insecure, and unbalanced mind.

Crommelynck molds his characters to fit into their phallus-obsessed world, underscoring in the most outlandish terms the lengths to which their twisted views may be carried. In Act II, for example, when Bruno is convinced that Stella is planning a tryst with an unknown lover, he forces her to wear a dark cloak and an ugly mask completely hiding her. What had been a paradisiac situation at the outset of the drama, results now in the creation of grotesque and deformed beings. These exaggerated creatures emerging from Crommelynck's pen are ugly and devoid of any redeeming feature. They are humorous in that they mirror to a great extent the notions concerning comedy set down by Cicero.

The province of the ridiculous lies within limits of ugliness and certain deformity; for the expressions are alone, or especially ridiculous which disclose and represent some ugliness in a not unseemly fashion.[2]

The grotesque is given a comic twist by exposing Bruno's progressively dismembered psyche for all to see. What had been united (Stella-Bruno) at the beginning of the drama has been severed at the end; what had been ethereal (the charming windmill Stella and Bruno had converted into their dream home) has become a sordid brothel-like domicile; what had been normal (sexuality in marriage) has become perverted.

Because of the pathological situation dramatized, Crommelynck's phallic celebration verges on the macabre. In this respect, *The Magnificent Cuckold* is reminiscent of Roger Vitrac's *Victor* (1928), in which a young man having been brought up to believe in his parents' purity learns, during the course of his adolescent years, that they were actually deceitful and hypocritical beings. Although Vitrac descends into the shadowy depths of his protagonists' psyches with verbal images, Crommelynck takes another route to gain similar results He allows free reign of emerging impulses to run their course. Both dramatists indulge in a kind of spasmodic dynamism that becomes a mechanical device after prolonged use: Victor candidly touches upon adultery, incest, insanity, and death; Bruno, in the warring scenes with his wife, destroys the once harmonious relationship. Both plays juxtapose the authentic, sincere, and beautiful child's world with the hypocritical and amoral realm of the adult.

Feelings of hostility, anxiety, uncertainty, and fear, suscitated by Crommelynck's reverse-reality procedure, are antithetical in their philosophical attitude to the ancient joyous comus. *The Magnificent Cuckold* is devoid of the charm and banter implicit in the plays of Crommelynck's contemporaries dealing with similar subjects: for example, *John of the Moon* (1929) by Marcel Achard, with its tender poetry and elusive fantasy universe, and Félicien Marceau's *The Good Soup* (1959), with its earthy sexuality. *The Magnificent Cuckold* is sardonic and bitter in temper, more like Dürrenmatt's brand of acidulous humor expressed in *The Physicists* and *The Meteor*

(1966). Dürrenmatt's characters are not only deeply disturbed about future events, but also feel continuously threatened by present living and thus seek refuge in a nightmarish and laughable realm of fantasy. In *Play Strindberg*, Dürrenmatt dramatizes the cruelty inherent in an ill-matched marriage: an irascible couple tortures each other to death in a mordant comedy routine. In "Preface to Four Plays," Dürrenmatt wrote:

Comedy alone is suitable for us. Our world has led to the grotesque as well as to the atom bomb, and so it is a world like that of Hieronymus Bosch whose apocalyptic paintings are also grotesque.[3]

Crommelynck's humor, like Dürrenmatt's, is caustic. It deals blows and counterblows against an ugly society, having no deep feeling for individuals or their private emotional aberrations. For Crommelynck and for Dürrenmatt, comedy is the only vehicle capable of concretizing and objectifying an inner structure.

Crommelynck stops at nothing when dramatizing his views. Whether his humor is raw or crude or overflows with instinctuality—it all serves his goal: to devaluate what he finds distasteful in the personal and collective world. He sees the dangers in an overly puritanical way of life as well as in an overly romantic and idealized realm. Bludgeoning, he mutilates his characters in the harshest of ways, verbally and viscerally. By disorienting the viewer, identification between audience and protagonist is no longer possible. Stella has become an antipathetic whore at the end; Bruno, unpleasantly insane no longer elicits any kind of pity, but annoyance and even anger. All are rejected along with the society they represent.

The theater as viewed by Crommelynck exposes openly and brutally unicentered views. Powerful dialogue and pulsating activities onstage attain paroxysmal force. The protagonists are caught up in a web, allowing themselves to be imprisoned by their instinctuality and their obsessive natures. Crommelynck's ability to ferret out the weakest aspect of his protagonist's personality, inflating and detaching it from the total human being, interweaves the result into a series of sequential situations to create a theatrical masterpiece. The abandon with which his underdeveloped characters express their monstrously absurd natures, kinetic emotions they arouse in each other, and the resulting situations, make the entire stage a viable entity. The phallus focus he achieves because of his well-developed sense of caricature depicts in startlingly abrasive terms one aspect of a general imbalance in his society, and perhaps within himself.

III   *Caricature*

Crommelynck's disturbing humor is based to a great extent on caricature. This technique, which succeeds in inflating certain patterns of behavior, results in disproportion in the play's framework, altering its dimension and focus. In so doing, the protagonists and the events depicted are taken out of the world of reality and placed in one of artifice. According to Bergson, caricature reveals an aspect of the author's psyche, a device marked with "insensibility" and "ulterior motive." It enables the dramatist to express in veiled terms his own feelings of superiority. The caricaturist, Bergson contends, like the puppeteer, can force his creatures to express the most excoriating emotions under the guise of folly. "The art of the caricaturist lies in his ability to seize that frequently imperceptible movement, and to make it visible for all to see by inflating it."[4]

Crommelynck uses caricature to condemn a general evil. In *The Magnificent Cuckold,* the drama emerges from the misuse of the phallus object and the resulting perverse emotional climate. Crommelynck considers his brittle, distorted characters the outgrowth of bigoted social attitudes. The unsalubrious inner climate of these maladjusted individuals is driven out into the open, delineated in sharp brushstrokes, and finally, to use André Breton's expression, emblazoned "for even the blindest to view."[5]

Caricature enables Crommelynck to express his own sense of revolt, his anger at society's hypocrisies. Under the guise of a carnival atmosphere, verbal games are indulged in by the protagonists. The entire substructure of *The Magnificent Cuckold* is built on chaos engendered by bitterness. Inner mechanisms are askew and

diabolical forces are in gestation. The contortions appearing in the
stage happenings—both visual and verbal—depict a kinetic climate
of ugliness.

Estrugo, the village scribe, is one of Crommelynck's finest caricatures. A blend of folly, wit, liveliness, fun, humor, and stupidity, he
is reminiscent of the stock character Bucco (Mouth) of Atellan satiric
drama. Although a kind of secretary, Estrugo's verbal transcriptions
become the catalyst of Bruno's own destruction. Estrugo (the
Mouth) keeps prattling throughout the drama, but is never believed
by Bruno—a bucco whose credibility is nil.[6] Estrugo was for Crommelynck, an "ambiguous double," a kind of devil figure; costumed
in whiteface and sneakers, he employed stylized gestures to excel as
a mime. His observations, transcribed by the fervor of his gestures,
succeeded in not depicting the truth of the situation, but in substan-
tiating Bruno's accusations and insinuations. Estrugo details the activities taking place between Petrus and Stella. As he looks through
the keyhole, he reports upon the sexual activities in verbal and
visual manner, he expresses his indignation and impatience by
bouncing up and down from a seated position, by thrusting his
hands in front of him in despair, and by casting his eyes to the
ground in dismay. Whatever the maneuver, his plastic gymnastics
fail to convince Bruno of Stella's innocence. Estrugo—the Mouth
and the Mime—becomes Bruno's vehicle for self-destruction, his
escape mechanism.

Just as Hogarth singled out the disreputable alcoholic in a series
of etchings entitled "Gin Lane"; Daumier, the lawyer who tried the
cases of the rich alone; and Doré who showed the monstrous in man, so
Crommelynck indulges in his verbal mutilations, thus giving free
reign to his resentments and hatreds. Bruno's treatment of Stella
and his all-consuming phallus-centered world, the result of society's
overevaluation of the notion of chastity, virginity, and spirituality,
were singled out for ridicule. Stella's cloak and cardboard mask
stood out in sharp contrast with the colorful and lively peasant costumes worn by the other participants. Her accessories lent an impersonal and timeless note to the play. She was no longer Stella,
Bruno's wife, but the village virgin or the village whore, the one
whose beauty and chastity (or lack of it) must remain hidden at all

costs. To make her ugly was Bruno's goal. The weight of the mask and cloak would render her stance awkward and ungainly, repelling men of her entourage. Stella thus was depersonalized and turned into an object devoid of feeling, jeered, mocked, ridiculed, ill-treated, and reviled. Gone was the beautiful joyous *commedia dell'arte* ingenue, the delightful young girl who in Italian comedy won the hearts of many men and whose lithe body and clever ways attracted and held her lover. Crommelynck's Stella is absurd: like the stock figure of Doric farces, as a collective phallus object, she is transformed into a prostitute type, vulgarized and shamed. Bruno, the manipulator of this incredible situation, is no longer the charming young lover of *comedia dell'arte plays*, but a man suffering from a sexual problem. He too achieves puppetlike dimensions: his mechanical personality indulges in the same antics and delusions, reacting as though he were dangling from a string, unable to gain a solid foothold on reality.

Crommelynck used the mask in this case to represent Bruno's attitude toward his wife. The *ugly* mask depicted Stella's *ugly* inner nature. Hence, the mask not only represented a psychological truth, as viewed by the protagonist, but became a vehicle for caricature—in both cases resembling Alfred Jarry's attitude on this subject. In "The Uselessness of Theater in the Theater," Jarry suggests that the mask points up the collective quality of the characters involved, imposing upon them a visual expression of a personality trait. In "Twelve Arguments on the Theater," he further declares that the dramatist who breathes life into his masked being creates a new existence; a fresh dynamism comes into being with the exteriorization of an inner conflict. The mask frees the forces within the personality that cannot be integrated, enabling them to crystallize on the stage and there to live out their lives in conflict or in harmony. Jean Genet's characters in *The Balcony* experience life only when wearing the mask of an archbishop, a general or a judge. In this disguise, another dimension of worldly experience is tapped: the limited realm of illusions is chosen as the field of encounter rather than the actual realm that spells boredom and disintegration. Beneath the mask, however, Genet's protagonists are like empty shells, shadow personalities. As Stella dons her mask, she loses her identity and becomes powerless to fight her battle. Interestingly, Bruno does not wear a mask but allows his mental attitude to serve the same purpose. It eclipses him from reality in a far more insidious manner. Like Genet's creatures who can function only with a mask (or in the world of illusion), so Bruno feels at home only in the fantasy realm he has erected for himself. In "Dogma for the New Masked Drama," O'Neill wrote, "One's outer life passes in the solitude haunted by the masks of others; one's inner life passes in the solitude hounded by the masks of oneself."[7]

Caricature enables Crommelynck to violate society's sexual taboos. Indeed, he rendered obscenity theatrically viable at a time when such enactments were forbidden. Stella's nurse and protector is certainly a throwback to the types featured in the farces that had been so popular during the Middle Ages. In these bawdy comedies—(eg. *The Sermon for a Marriage* by Roger de Colleyre or *Farce of the Prince of Fools* by Pierre Gringoire)—everything, from pope to king, is acceptable for ridicule. In *The Magnificent Cuckold,* the nurse, being powerless to guard her mistress's morals, enters the frenetic madness ensuing onstage, thus releasing her own tensions and those of the other protagonists.[8]

Crommelynck's expert use of caricature enables him to heighten or to slacken the play's pace, therefore controlling its suspense. He stresses the *lazzi* aspect of *The Magnificent Cuckold*: extreme action that forever generates excitement and sparks madness. When the cowherd enters, the idyllic and romantic opening lines suddenly change to hectic activity. Stella is forced to fight off the intruder. The rough-and-tumble gestures that ensue (always centered around phallus-oriented desires) are so speedily enacted, including clouts bandied about, that a kaleidoscopic atmosphere is achieved. Such speed injected into the stage happenings is reminiscent of Futurist canvases by Balla and Severini. These served to underscore the ultramotility of modern society. When the count comes after Stella, another, less lively, stage battle ensues in which the elegance of the count's gestures and Stella's earthy manner set off a plebeian versus aristocratic approach to sex. Petrus's sexual prowess, described in detail by Estrugo, is humorous in that it activates the salivary glands of the listeners. Speed and an overt sense of jocularity are achieved again in the last scene when the young men of the village run after Stella and tear at her clothes, expressing the urgency of their desires. They are truly the inheritors of the Greek comus: theirs is a veritable celebration of earthy ways expressed through leaping and running incited by sexual conquest.

No matter how humorous or ribald the outcome of the caricature, Crommelynck's goal is, perhaps unconsciously, to disfigure and unmask ideations imposed upon man by society. Freud declared that caricature was a means of rejecting those who stand for "authority and respect and who are exalted in some sense."[9] Although Crommelynck was the product of a traditional upbringing with the usual constricting and stultifying forces corroding his freedom of spirit, he sought to break down the barriers he felt stunted his emotional growth. He certainly succeeded on a theatrical level and used the caricature as his chief weapon.

IV *The Psychology of Jealousy*

Toulouse-Lautrec singled out Yvette Guilbert's nose for ridicule in his caricatures; Crommelynck chose an emotional sickness: jealousy. Unlike Euripides' Medea, Shakespeare's Othello, or Molière's Arnolphe in *School for Wives*, Crommelynck's Bruno is unique in that he represents the extreme of a monomaniacal jealousy—perhaps more humorous and less pathetic a being than those dramatized by his predecessors. Bruno's sickness, a jealousy not based on fact, emerges as a distortion of reality and a vehicle to further destroy his happiness. Bruno's is "a case of total jealousy";[10] though Estrugo has frequently been compared to Shakespeare's Iago, any similarity between the two is coincidental. Iago is evil: he plans Othello's downfall. Estrugo is a kind of "fool" who tells the truth, but in such a way as to sustain Bruno's torment, as a kind of countertruth. Because Bruno's jealousy is founded on his own mental ravages, and Othello's on Iago's planned deceptions, Shakespeare's creation elicits pathos and brings about tragedy, whereas Crommelynck's results in an outcome suitable to the aberration.

Bruno's desperation may be said to arise from the sense of despair that follows what he believes to be the shattering of an ideal world: the imagined perfection with which he has imbued his love object.

His attitude toward love is strictly adolescent, indicating his childlike view of perfect marital bliss. Stella and Bruno, children playing at the game of marriage, have never emerged from a paradisiac situation. Even their home, a transformed wind-mill with whitewashed walls surrounded by a beautiful flower garden, gives the impression of ordered perfection. Life in all of its beauty appears to be unfolding.

When adolescents like Bruno and Stella fall in love, the object of their desire seems perfect. No evaluation or objectivity has come into being to mar the completeness of their vision of each other or of the world. What Bruno sees in Stella is a projection of his *anima*; what she sees in her husband is a projection of her *animus*. The anima may be defined as an autonomous complex that represents man's unconscious inner attitude toward the woman; the animus is the woman's unconscious view of the man. Because Bruno's ego (or that aspect of his conscious attitude) was not strong enough to relate to his anima objectively, he identified with it and so it remained unconscious. Stella suffered the same fate. Both protagonists were victims of their anima and animus projections respectively; hence they would be doomed to suffer the disappointments of those who never succeeded in detaching the objects of their projections from their unconscious. Since Bruno's ego experiences no objectivity in his situation, he loses all perspective and becomes the tool and victim of his anima. He cannot build a relationship with his beloved because he never becomes aware of her existence as a human being, nor can he distinguish reality from illusion. Had he been able to objectify his complex, it could have been depotentiated. His ego then would have emerged and the energy dispensed trying to possess his object and the urgency needed to achieve his goal would have diminished.

Stella was the bearer of Bruno's anima image. As the beautiful, radiant, fresh, sincere, tender, and ideal soul, she struggled to play his game, to further his illusions, believing erroneously that if she yielded, he would be cured. Bruno and Stella, childhood sweethearts, knew no conflict. Stella, having never experienced anything but harmony with Bruno, did not know the meaning of confrontation. Unaware at first of Bruno's delusions, she did not understand to what extent they had encroached upon his conscious frame of reference. Undeveloped herself, though far healthier than he, she acquiesced to his ruling and sacrificed herself to sexual martyrdom. First she gave herself to Petrus, then yielded to many men. The situation grew so pathetic, so ridiculous, that it finally aroused Stella's anger. The idyllic world of the early months of their marriage she knew could never be recaptured: the warmth, confidence, and protective atmosphere of newborn love had given way to deceit and perversion. In Act III the stage happenings were transformed into a mad carnival scene where folly and lust predominated. Stella rejected her husband's masochistic views and decided she would become what he considered her to be—unfaithful. The whirligig, to use Jean-Paul Sartre's word, was over.

Bruno's jealousy went beyond the usual obsessive fear of losing the love object. The fact that he described his wife's body in detail to everyone in ecstatic outpourings indicated an inclination for *voyeurism* and masochism. Suspicion seemed his *raison d'être* and he created situations to feed his sick psyche. He required Stella to deceive him:

I want you impure and I want to be dishonored! Let there be no compromise. I'll be a cuckold this very day or I'll be dead. Horns or cord. Choose for me.

Nevertheless, he did not believe in her infidelity.

She makes believe she's obeying me so that I won't further my investigations! But I have my own ideas on the subject: find out! The one she cherishes, she won't accept under my very eyes. Misfortune to the one who does not come.

When Lugné-Poë created the role of Bruno, he saw him as a libidinous lecher, a "giant, erotic clown," a "sexually obsessed" individual who was forever "eating Stella with his eyes" and "beating her while trembling with wantonness."[11] Lugné-Poë understood the morbid side of a man who had become prey to demons, who had stepped over that "shadowy line" from sanity to madness. It was for this reason that some of his repartees were spoken with such force as to resemble a series of "striking fist marks" aimed at both protagonists and spectators. Variety, too, was implicit in his portrayal: there were moments of desperate lyricism, deep emotion, and a tenderness that "verged on the sublime."[12]

The humor of the situations in this comedy of errors is pathological. It is based on Bruno's blindness and macabre behavior pattern. Bruno's code of ethics spells the deep-seated neurosis of a man who seeks to create problems and cannot live without pain. Bruno the masochist is incapable of experiencing pleasure and seeks humiliation and suffering. The Roman ethic of strength, courage, and fortitude has been abandoned in favor of one based on anguish. Such a pathetic creature was immortalized in the nineteenth-century Pierrot, the clown whose tears perpetually flowed, telling pathos in his every feature.[13]

The energy used by Bruno to gain control over his outer environment by ordering Stella to wear a cloak and mask and forcing her to have liaisons could have been put to better use had it flowed inward strengthening his ego. Because the psychic energy was withdrawn from his inner world and projected outward, it increased his inadaptability to his environment. Bruno thus could be labeled a kind of "renegade" type who gives up the struggle; a psychological deserter such as Tennyson's "Lotus-Eater."[14]

> Let us alone. What pleasure can we have
> To war with evil?

Bruno's "slothful" and passive ways allow him to eclipse himself from reality. Unwilling or unable to alter his attitude toward life, he negates any kind of heroism and is conquered by his own negativity. It could be said he married his obsession, psychologically speaking, and allowed himself to be victimized by it.

To underscore the infantile side of the protagonists, Crommelynck uses the technique expertly employed by Jean Cocteau in *The Children of the Game* and by Jean Genet in *The Maids*; the game ritual becomes an intrinsic part of plot and character. At first, Bruno's and Stella's games are innocent enough. They speak in their own mysterious love talk; they play hide and seek, they converse with the animals, flowers, trees, and plants, living beings in their own animistic universe. As the game ritual gains momentum, it may be likened to the perverted love games delineated in Cocteau's and Genet's works. What had been purported to be lively banter becomes a sexual battle of hatred and invectiveness. With erotic fervor, Bruno listens to Estrugo's account of Petrus's lovemaking; later, he enters into complicity with the young men who pour over Stella, delighting in this sensual sport. Like Cocteau's characters, Stella and Bruno enjoy their games in their private universe, a place of mystery and magic understood and enjoyed only by children. They also have their fetishes, but not those used in *The Children of the Game* (pins, boxes, old programs or in *The Maids*, gloves, statues, letters); their own animistic hierophants are those of ancient societies—trees, grass, flowers, birds—all transformed by the protagonists' imagination into spiritual and sensual forces. Whether dramatized by Cocteau, Genet, or Crommelynck, in the world of children, the game makes manifest certain undercurrents and unregenerate emotions. A love-hate relationship enables the participants to escape from the unacceptable world of reality into one of illusion. Crommelynck understood this quality of the game. He, therefore, infused his protagonists with gusto, pain, and confusion. Each succeeded in his own way: Stella opted for sensual delights and Bruno for his childlike regressive world.

V *A Kinetic Constructivist Production*

The Moscow production in 1922 of *The Magnificent Cuckold*, directed by Vsevolod Meyerhold, with sets by L. P. Popova, was praised in newspapers the world over for its innovations in acting techniques, stage design, lighting, and directing.

Meyerhold's production stressed the humor and boldness of caricature, while simultaneously underscoring the world of illusion and earthiness. The Russian director rejected the realistic theater of Stanislavsky in favor of a new reality that sought to arouse the spectators' emotions and imagination. For Meyerhold, theater was not designed merely to entertain an aristocratic public, featuring plays with "langorous recitatives" or idealizations of vacuous societies;

rather, he sought to concretize revolutionary goals of the new Russia. To achieve this effect, he abolished the stage curtain as had Lugné-Poë and Paul Fort in France. He extended, as they had, the proscenium arch out into the audience so that an interchange could take place more closely between spectator and actor. He also constructed, as had Jacques Copeau of the Vieux-Colombier theater, mobile forms on a bare stage in lieu of decors, thus accentuating the temporal quality of the atmosphere. He rejected suspended decors and theatrical arches and so allowed action to take place outside of the "scenic cage." Similar to Jacques Copeau and his disciples, for Meyerhold each play was an individual blending of gesture, movement, and speech. His method, described as the "technique of biomechanics," may be set forth as follows.

The whole technique of biomechanics lies in the careful study of the time of preparation for a certain action: of the emotional and physical state of the moment of action itself: and the resulting anticlimax of reaction.[15]

Gestures and body movements had to be precise and in keeping with the personality portrayed. The intonations and emerging emotions would then find their natural equivalents and the actors would be able to coordinate the means at their disposal to express their character's "excitability."[16]

Meyerhold used his acting area three-dimensionally: the actor was no longer isolated on the stage but participated in the general flow of rhythmic and spacial dynamics generated by a harmonious combination of body, scenery, and accessories. When Meyerhold produced Verhaeren's play *Dawns* (1920), he used "a whole scale of flat surfaces, practicables, and cubes of different heights, joined by steps and inclined planes."[17] His directives to L. P. Popova, the creator of the stage apparatus for *The Magnificent Cuckold*, resulted in a concretization of the restless energy inherent in Crommelynck's protagonists.

Popova was a Constructivist. Unlike the Cubists, who broke down objects in terms of form and used movement as a means of expressing mass, the Constructivists were anti-aesthetic. They used raw materials for their creations that were designed to be functional and utilitarian, thus blending political beliefs ("the soul and ideals of the workers") with artistic creativity.[18] Constructivism originated in Russia around 1913 and its main supporters were Malevich, Tatlin, Rodchenko, and Popova. It consisted of circles, diagonals, and rectangles applied to a blank background. Each design was to impress itself into the spacial form in question in perfect proportion and balance, each line representing an organic mass in terms of motion, color, and texture.

For *The Magnificent Cuckold* the stage setting was based on the following principles outlined by Meyerhold:

1. Three-dimensional linear construction.
2. Visual rhythm determined by the effects that were neither pictorial nor set in relief.
3. The inclusion in the construct of only those "active" parts necessary for the actor's activities.[19]

In order to situate the scene in some temporal domain, Meyerhold suggested that Popova build a wheel, since Crommelynck's stage directions said that the play took place in a converted wind-mill. The lively colors Popova used in the design of the wheel would help audiences and actors experience the rotary sensation of the mill while giving the entire scene a kaleidoscopic effect.

Popova's construct consisted of black, tab, and red multiform pedestals made up of circles, stairs, ladders, doors, squares, rectangles, and parallels. Each was an organic entity in itself, each an expression of the actor's kineticism, each organizing space in terms of rhythmic and plastic dimensions. The stage was active and diametrically opposed to the conventional decors used in Parisian productions. Lighting focused only on the stage areas where activity occurred, thus opposing light-dark spacial areas, which injected a more dynamic impress into the proceedings. The actors wore mainly the workingman's blue apron—"work clothes" and distinguishing accessories were added to each character's costume, as Meyerhold wrote, in keeping with his role.

Popova's large and complicated stage apparatus was used in its entirety when groups filled the proscenium, and in separate sections when one or two actors came onstage. As the actors jumped, fell, or disappeared, they performed on the various parts of the construct, which was superbly adaptable. Each element of the setting played a dual role: as a single bench, window, incline, and as part of a totality—the massive object viewed as a whole.[20]

Popova's scheme was in perfect keeping with the ebullience of the adolescent psyches of the protagonists. Viewed either as a utilitarian object to serve actors and playwrights or as a giant toy to mirror the protagonists' anthropoid psyche, it remained a memorable achievement in theater design.

Meyerhold's emphasis on the visual dimension of *The Mganificent Cuckold* created a kind of macrostructure in which the protagonists lived their solitary as well as their collective roles. The new universe that came into being—an agglomeration of figurations—was action personified, triggering off a continuous series of emotional collisions. The spectacle became an awakening process through the word as well as the visual experience.

The Magnificent Cuckold remained Crommelynck's greatest success. George Pioch called it "a work of genius"; Maurice Rostand, "unique in the annals of the theater," one of "the most powerful studies in jealousy"; and Marcel Lapierre, "a play of monumental proportion."[21]

CHAPTER 4

The Puerile Lovers:
Illusion Versus Reality (1921)

T HE *Puerile Lovers,* written between 1911 and 1913, was produced by Firmin Gémier on March 4, 1921, at the Théâtre de
la Comédie Montaigne. Gaston Baty's mise-en-scène was lauded by
the critics as was the play itself and its stars, Fernand Crommelynck
and Berthe Bady. The performances, however, were shortlived due
to the unexpected death of the female lead.

A slow-paced work, powerful in its simplicity, *The Puerile Lovers*
is violent in the emotions it engenders. It dramatizes the conflicts
encountered by individuals who cannot face reality and who choose
instead a world of illusion. Crommelynck offers no panaceas. Life is
a degrading experience even for the happiest of individuals. Joy is
short-lived; physical beauty is evanescent; the body is doomed to
decay. The precarious nature of man's physical world is brought into
sharp relief by the symbolism of Crommelynck's images—water,
mirrors, moon, glass—each in its own way reinforcing an atmosphere of utter solitude even when these feelings of loneliness are
momentarily camouflaged by one exceptional love experience.

I *The Plot*

The Puerile Lovers revolves around Princess Elisabeth de
Groulingen and Baron Jean Louis Frédéric Cazou. When young,
they were the talk of Europe. Their love had become legendary for
its beauty and the joy it exuded. The play opens in the living room of
the Triton Villa, with a view of the sea. Baron Cazou is no longer a
handsome, strong, and dashing young man; he is now old, senile,
and numb with rheumatism. Neither is Elisabeth the exquisite

65

dream creature of years past; however, she refuses to accept her decrepitude and wears long gowns to cover her body, heavy makeup, and a veil to hide her wrinkles. She is convinced that in this way she is able to "deceive the mirrors." Elisabeth lives exclusively in the past, in a remote realm of perfection and idealism. Her world of fantasy is embodied by a lover, l'Etranger (the Stranger), a thirty-year-old man who has been pursuing her for months. He is the reincarnation of the youthful Cazou. When in the company of l'Etranger, Elisabeth is alluded to as l'Etrangère (female Stranger); then she plays the role of the coquettish young girl she had once been. Insofar as Elisabeth is concerned, time seems to have been immobilized, past events and joys are relived. But time is still fleeting and we watch the old Cazou's physical and spiritual disintegration. A paralleling situation of the legendary lovers (Elisabeth and Cazou) is that of fourteen-year-old Marie-Henriette and her beloved Walter, aged fifteen. They adore each other, but their parents forbid them to keep company and they can meet only in secret. Out of desperation Walter begs Marie-Henriette to follow him to the sea—to his world of perfection. L'Etrangère encourages the young girl to be lulled into submission by Walter. Life cannot offer the happiness l'Etrangère's ideal world conjures forth. Marie-Henriette finally yields and a double suicide follows. L'Etrangère can no longer stand the tension between her world of illusion and the reality of her pitiful condition. She must know whether L'Etranger loves her for what she is or whether he adores the image she has created for him. Hence, she removes her veil and makeup. L'Etranger looks at her—and vanishes in sorrow. Elisabeth crumbles to the floor.

II *Illusion and Reality*

The conventions that help individuals accept the ravages of time and survive such destructive forces have been rejected by Elisabeth. Her unwillingness to experience nature's course has engendered within her psyche a complex network of emotions ranging from bitterness and rancor to disgust, fear, and love. She lives in an unsteady world of shifting excesses, of illusion and reality, the image and its reflection. Because her inner struggle is so extreme it may be viewed as an expression of a basic antagonism toward life. Unwilling to follow the dictates of nature in its birth-death course, pitifully weak in her struggle against an implacable destiny, Elisabeth seeks refuge and consolation in a world that lies beyond the temporal— where reality gives way to phantasmagoria.

Princess Elisabeth de Groulingen was modeled after a woman Crommelynck had once met at Ostend when he was in his twenties. She was the wife of an ambassador from a northern country. To Crommelynck, this woman of thirty-five was already old. In his imagination he saw her as having once been beautiful and as having experienced a most perfect love that had slowly come to a halt with age.[1] Crommelynck was traumatized by what he took to be a living example of nature's destructive ways. For the first time, the meaning of age, senility, and death came into focus for him. *The Puerile Lovers* may be looked upon as a projection of Crommelynck's own struggle to accept the ravages of time.

A mortuary atmosphere prevails in the drama as Elisabeth—like the veiled Isis—wanders about in her necropolis. By gaining sustenance exclusively from her optical illusions, from the glitter of her beautiful gowns, she displays an inability and an unwillingness to adapt to the transformatory process in nature. Her need for escape has grown into a psychosis and a renunciation of life. The world she has created for herself and the phantasms she lives are stultifying. She has become a prisoner of her own regressive domain, a childlike universe in which there is room only for beauty, tenderness, and love. Life for her is bitter and corrosive when away from her dream. Elisabeth thus is a psychological cripple who limps through the three acts, never understanding the implications of her destructive attitude for herself and for those surrounding her. She is a lonely shadow.

Crommelynck increases the tension in Elisabeth's world by juxtaposing her fantasy realm with the existing situation: age with youth and object with function. As the breach grows wider, her illusory love relationship with L'Etranger assumes the stature of a Platonic abstraction, an ideal: unattainable perfection. L'Etranger fulfills all of her needs, prayers, and dreams. In the grip of her fantasy world, the erosion of her physical being is momentarily eclipsed; but when the workaday world intrudes, her pain grows excruciating. Then she allows herself to be cradled by l'Etranger's tender love phrases. Every now and then her senile dyspeptic husband comes onstage and she is forced to listen to his meaningless cacophonies. He is a useless remnant of a bygone era, a living carcass, and his presence haunts her like a nightmare. When her suffering becomes unbearable, delineations between illusion and reality grow hazy; discernment vanishes.

Crommelynck's use of antithetical stage situations heightens the protagonist's plight and thus aids to bring events to a climax. Although Elisabeth yearns for eternal youth and hides her shriveled body, she is aware of her acts; therefore, her schizophrenic conduct becomes a pose. Her personality is consciously fragmented; her notions are willfully dislocated; her ways grow increasingly pitiful. Elisabeth's double life, or her dual vision, causes parasitic relationships and unregenerate situations. Crommelynck further stresses her pathetic mental outlook with a series of images (glass, water, wind), each representing in one way or another the splintered, liquid, and ephemeral world of her disenchanted realm.

When becoming l'Etrangère, Elisabeth dons an elegant costume, wig, and gloves: but lives in the shadows to conceal the signs of decrepitude. She confesses to Marie-Henriette, her youthful counterpart, the conscious efforts she has made to bring a new dimension into existence, erect a world based on love and beauty.

I alone know the care I took in trying to deceive the mirrors! I fear light, and the wind, and the rain, which would ruin my makeup! . . . It's terrible, isn't it? I don't dare lift up my veil anymore and I wait for night in order to cry! Console me. (p. 173)

Darkness and concealment increase the distance between the world Elisabeth fabricates and the one of which she is unfortunately a part. Her rejection of the elements (light, water, wind, rain) is symptomatic of her flight from realism. Although Elisabeth is aware of her futile need to escape truth, she persists in her game because it is the only way she is able to function.

My eyes were not this clear, their color has been spent . . . And if you saw my hands, under the gloves, my poor hands! you would pity me, certainly . . . The rings have fallen off my fingers—one by one. I'll give them to you if you want them.

Once, I had been so beautiful . . . My great pain stems from this, my regret is born from this . . . I thought it was sufficient to be beautiful!

I do not regret this or that part of my past, but now my days are without adventure, days . . . Life was happy. When I walked, I seemed to be airborne . . . (p. 173)

Elisabeth seems hypnotized by the mirrors surrounding her living room, fascinated by the image they project. Like Narcissus, she becomes obsessed with her reflection, neglecting the inner being. And her mask succeeds in misleading her momentarily. Impassable and implacable, she gives the impression of having transcended all conflict within her, and of having overcome the cleavage between the fantasy and the real worlds. At times her identification with her mask seems complete. The mirrors will repeat *ad infinitum* her veiled visage in countless nuances. Yet, her inner world, hidden from view, festers in darkness. It becomes increasingly confused and disconnected.

An instrument of self-contemplation, the mirror reflects the outer state, the world that dazzles and attracts. The glitter of Elisabeth's vestments mesmerizes at first and absorbs the magic quality she seeks to instill about her. In the mirror her beauty gives the impression of being alive, and this intangible entity succeeds in captivating the unsuspecting Etranger. As used by Elisabeth, the mirror has become a vehicle capable of prolonging her fantasy world and being a buffer against unhappiness. Unlike Jean Cocteau in *Orpheus* and Lewis Carroll in *Alice Through the Looking Glass*, who used mirrors as instruments permitting access into another world, Elisabeth's fetish locks her into an arcane realm. Because the mirror image has immobilized Elisabeth in its reflection, because it fixes her in its contours, she is transformed into a cold and calculating entity comparable to Mallarmé's mirror fetish.

> O mirror!
> Your ennui framed in cold iced-over water . . .
> *(O miroir!*
> *Eau froide par l'ennui dans ton cadre gêlée.)*

The words Elisabeth speaks to l'Etranger are warm and passionate; however, they resound throughout the play in sharp contrast to the lifeless image she has created of herself: an idea given form.

The intensity of the love sequences between l'Etranger and l'Etrangère serve to create a double theatrical vision. As the play opens, Elisabeth's imagined and real worlds are relatively compatible. But as events move forward, the two worlds become viciously antagonistic, and the interplay between l'Etranger and l'Etrangère grows more abrasive. The two shadow personalities trigger off a series of chain reactions, involuntary memory sequences in both chronological and analogical patterns. The worlds conjured into existence at this point are microstructures of what had been experienced in a linear past. As l'Etrangère reintegrates her former existence (as Elisabeth) into the present and confronts Cazou, creating a complex of symbiotic relationships between the protagonists, a dramatic collage imbricates the events, expanding the worlds (both real and imagined) and at the same time disorienting the individuals. The increasing psychological confusion of the characters and the growing unsteadiness of their ways causes the two worlds and their time sequences to come into collision.

Confrontation, however, does not always mean growth. None of the characters in *The Puerile Lovers* evolve. Elisabeth will always live in her concocted childlike realm. "I would like everything to be happy," she says (p. 206). She needs a world divested of responsibilities, conflict, and sadness. An enemy of life, Elisabeth becomes the foe of transformation and growth—a foe of the earth principle.

I was disconsolate because everything on earth is just too finite. Since I realized this, my happiness has always been blended with regret (p. 207).

For Elisabeth, the earth is heaven's enemy. The earth is mortal, subject to change, ugliness, dissolution; it gives and takes life. Heaven is the domain of the eternal, changeless, spiritual world. It is remote, all-encompassing, a container of hyperspace or transspace. Heaven is the only world to which Elisabeth can escape and can fulfill her desire for happiness.

Although Elisabeth does not evolve in the true sense of the word, the growing awareness of the dichotomy between her phantasmagorias and her life situation makes her existence untenable. An impasse is reached at the finale of the drama. As the love sequences with l'Etranger grow more passionate, as his demands upon her become more imperative, she feels, paradoxically, the need to reveal her true self. She must know whether l'Etranger loves her true self or the illusion, the mirror image. As the risk involved becomes more pressing, her terror increases, and the intensity of her emotions heightens. Removing her mask, she does away with artifice and braves danger. In true Pirandellian style, she seeks to make the world of appearances come true—with one great difference. Pirandello's schizophrenic characters, Henrico IV and those in *Right You Are*, for the most part are unaware of the ambiguity existing in their worlds. The demarcation lines between illusion and reality are no longer clearly defined. For Elisabeth, however, the dichotomy is painfully acute and thus makes her torment more abrasive.

As long as l'Etranger sees only Elisabeth's vestments (veil, makeup, gloves, wig, elegant gowns), he sings her praises and looks upon her ineffable countenance as the most exquisite of forms. She is his soul mate, his ideal. Gazing at the vast expanse of water that covers the horizon, he describes his vision and his love in tantalizing nocturnal glimmers.

The moon has slowly extinguished all the globes of the dikes. You see, heaven and sea appear to me as though from the depths of a magic mirror. I am so far away, so near you, Elisabeth!

To sail endlessly toward the horizon, in this small boat whose green fire frequently extinguishes itself (p. 212).

L'Etranger longs for the land of enchantment, for the fairy-tale atmosphere and unknown climes—sidereal worlds.

Here man feels himself forever carried away by the current of the heavenly bodies, the winds, the tides, so close, yet always so distant! (p. 212)

The servants intrude upon Elisabeth's dreamworld. They prod her to find the truth, not for altruistic reasons, but because of their essentially vicious natures. They want her to suffer and l'Etranger to leave. They taunt her and threaten her. When l'Etranger arrives, they drop hints about her age every now and then. They swoop into the lives of l'Etranger and l'Etrangère like harpies, bringing fear and torment in their wake. Elisabeth's will to deceive seems to totter. "If you love me," she says to l'Etranger, "you will not open your eyes." Yet, she knows she cannot prolong the optical illusion: all must come to an end.

The finale is brought about rather abruptly. The senile Cazou returns from a walk and looks frantically about the living room for his shadow, "the only thing he has left." In a sequence marked with irony, Cazou refers to his shadow as a friendly animal and starts feeding it sugar: "Only it loves him now" (p. 219). Shuffling about the table trying to grab hold of his shadow, he stammers half sentences, launches into his past, and recalls his love for Elisabeth and his own happy youth. L'Etranger, the younger version of Cazou, expresses his admiration at the mention of the legendary couple and asserts:

And I was shown the trace of your steps on the side of snowy mountaintops, above the clouds and on the beaches, along the four seas. "The Princess and Count Cazou!" And once, your initials were engraved in the bark of a tree, in a virtually unknown forest: so powerful was this impression that all the shadows on earth were for me a replica of your love! (p. 221)

Strangely enough, l'Etranger and Cazou—youth and age—seem to merge. As l'Etranger speaks in rapturous tones of the princess to Cazou, the old count too, pronounces her name as if speaking of a divinity. The world of shadows now diminishes and blinding lights inundate the stage. Elisabeth and l'Etranger move about in circular patterns; their words resound, reverberate, and collide in a semi-dream atmosphere. They are at the same time connected and disjointed from each other as spatial configurations take hold of the stage areas. When l'Etranger gazes at his beloved, now illuminated by the harsh light of consciousness, he is overwhelmed. He sees her discolored lips, heavy eyelids, white hair, and her brittle and wrinkled skin. She has ceased to be the beautiful creature of his dreams, but is ugliness personified, and the sight is more than he can bear. Indescribable pity overwhelms him. He walks out, still searching for the image of beauty he had carried about in his heart for these long months. Solitary in her decrepitude, Elisabeth, now a tragic and grotesque figure, collapses. Her world has shriveled. It is as dry and as lifeless as her body. Illusion had been an empty shell, as superficial as the person she had created for herself.

III   *The Senex Figure*

Interesting in *The Puerile Lovers* is Crommelynck's view of the senex figure. Crommelynck sees the old man as senile, awkward, and revolting—no longer venerated as the wise father or the archetypal figure of antiquity. Cazou is a horrid specimen of decrepitude, a wreck, reviled by his servants and degraded by his wife. He also suffers from amnesia and has forgotten his youth and one great love. Obliterating this love, which is Elisabeth's *raison d'être*, and which she spends her entire life trying to resurrect, is an afront to her being and reason enough for her hostility toward him.

Count Cazou represents a disintegrated personality. He stands for death. Unlike those positive senex figures of the past (e.g. Tiresias), who prefigured a new order, fresh attitudes, and rebirth, Crommelynck's view of age resembles Samuel Beckett's. In *End Game*, for example, age does not mean a future *renovatio*. Cazou's infirmity lets no new element enter into the picture; each generation (Cazou and Elisabeth, l'Etranger and l'Etrangère, Marie-Henriette and Walter) continues in its perpetual decline.

In *The Puerile Lovers* the senex figure is inoperative except as a *shadow* personality, as attested to in the guise of l'Etranger. But here, too, only a past, in a figurative sense, comes into existence. Repetition in a continually declining situation is l'Etranger's fate. To underscore Crommelynck's nihilistic view, words such as *rot* and *decay* permeate the dialogue when associated with the senex figure: "Ha! rot! rot! rot! Boiled monkey! Phuah" (p. 133). Anger, resentment, and hatred for the state of feebleness resound throughout the drama.

Words such as *young* and *old, illusion* and *reality* are set apart.
Elisabeth rejects the harsh facts of life and yearns for the golden age
of youth. But such a disposition is heavy, burdensome, and infertile.
In keeping with the play's negativism, symbols of futurity are also
omitted. The young die, swallowed by the waters of an unquench-
able maw. Sexuality is nowhere to be found. Melancholia sweeps
through the atmosphere, gripping each of the protagonists in an
inextricable vise. Princess Elisabeth or, to use an allegorical term,
Dame Melancholy, represents an unregenerate *senex* consciousness. Disintegration in body leads to disintegration of the mind and
with it senescence, a downgrading of life and a dying complex. The
Zeitgeist is regressive; decomposition is taking over. Crommelynck's
characters are unlike Ionesco's in *Amédée or How to Get Rid of It*,
where despite the growth of a corpse and proliferating mushrooms
the protagonists emerge from the putrefaction into light and freedom. There is no possibility of a second beginning. Man is not to be
born again.

IV *Water Symbolism*

The Puerile Lovers is a symbolic drama. Concrete objects stand
for intangible forces or ideas, whereas images embody interrelated
meanings and sensations. Maurice Maeterlinck's plays *The Intruder*
and *The Blind*, which stress the mysterious world of death, blindness, and second sight, clearly influenced Crommelynck. In
Maeterlinck's dramas, moods pave the way for the creation of an
inner reality on the stage, for a ritualistic pacing of events and
dialogue. In Maeterlinck's dramas as well as in *The Puerile Lovers*, a
static effect is created; a mystical world comes into being where
feeling tones and a kind of implacable and corrosive Greek fatality
reign. As was the case of many symbolic dramas (e.g. *Axel* by Villiers
de l'Isle Adam, 1890), the invisible world was concretized on the
stage by poetic images that had to be deciphered by the audience.
Stage structures were often lugubrious, heavy, and portentous. The
droaning tonalities of Villiers de l'Isle Adam's poetic prose, and the
chiaroscuro of the lighting effects, comparable to Teniers' land-

scapes, underscored the pathetic nature of man pitted against overwhelming cosmic forces.

Symbolic theater as expressed in the works of Maeterlinck, Villiers de l'Isle Adam, and Crommelynck makes use of evocative,
suggestive, vague, and subtle nuances. A *romantic* vision, to use
Mme de Staël's phrase, prevails, in contrast to Marivaux's and Musset's capricious and hallucinatory worlds—realms in which clarity,
cleverness, and sardonic humor are *de rigueur*. *The Puerile Lovers*
follows in the Gérard de Nerval tradition where "The dream world
is a second life." Crommelynck's characters intuit their sorrow and
feel their pain. In order to survive, if only momentarily, they crush
the constricting boundaries of old-type reality, the logical and linear
world in which they believe themselves to be prisoners. Answers
are not conclusive and security does not exist.

Crommelynck's symbolic theater—its substructure based on an
interplay of concrete and abstract worlds—was popular at the turn of
the century. The rejection of Naturalist and Realist playwrights,
such as Brieux, Goncourt, Becque, and the search for arcane
realms, as exemplified in the poems of Mallarmé, Verlaine, and
Laforgue, mirrored the discoveries taking place in the medical
world. Doctors Liébault, Bernheim, and Janet were delving into the
unconscious; Charcot was carrying out his experiments in hysteria at
the Salpétrière in Paris. (Freud was his student and became fascinated by the revelations he witnessed.) Bergson's *Time and Free
Will* and *Matter and Memory* pointed to the limits of rational thinking and played up intuition as a means of seizing the source of being.

The Puerile Lovers stirred the arcane realm of symbols, images,
and the sensations that pictorial visions arouse. The house in the
play is named "The Triton Villa." The living room, with its large bay
window, has a view out upon the sea. The stage directions give the
distinct impression that the drama is being enacted on some kind of
oasis—a sandbank, maybe—that has risen up from the depths of the
sea and will sink back into its waters at the end of the play.

Water is perhaps the most important image in *The Puerile Lovers*.
Unlike in "The Drunken Ship" of Rimbaud, water is not looked
upon as a source of life and nourishment or as a replenishing and

purifying force. It is a trap. It is an indifferent mass representing infinite possibilities, a preformal world of virtualities that may never be materialized. Crommelynck's water images are destructive throughout. They envelop, absorb, and dissolve individuals. They lead to drowning, forgetfulness, and hallucinatory or fanciful existences that fragment, psychologically, those who come into contact with them. Thus, water encourages a return to some nebulous beginning—without hope of rebirth. A regressive force, water becomes a vehicle for putrefaction. It numbs and effaces. In Crommelynck's view water is fearsome. It ravages like wind and tornadoes, which are also mentioned in the play's dialogue. Like these natural phenomena, water is an evil omen, the harbinger of death, and a force that has lured fishermen to their demise. Water is chaos.

Marie-Henriette and Walter (*wa*-l-*ter*) are personifications of water. Similar to this liquid element, their love is preformal; it has not yet solidified. Water, therefore, is a potential force in the drama that emerges and vanishes in rhythm with the young people's encounters and with their differences with the other protagonists. Marie-Henriette and Walter are like l'Etranger and l'Etrangère—shadow figures, portents of what could come into existence. Their love perhaps could have been indestructible had it been given the chance to evolve. But their love was stifled by their parents who denigrated the young couple's passion. L'Etrangère urges Marie-Henriette not to realize her happiness, to allow it to remain illusion. Once love is experienced, this fire has been ignited, it burns itself out leaving only charred remains. As water figures, neither Marie-Henriette nor Walter have the solidity to fight the older generation, the stamina to lash back at nature's cyclical force. Their dream of perfection, of "ideal" love, of understanding, is doomed from the outset. Reality is always disappointing for water people.

When Walter first visits Marie-Henriette, his voice is robust and direct. Then, as the older generation begins castigating their relationship, his strength diminishes. His voice grows remote; the sounds of wind and of the seas take over. The hypnotic melodies of the sirens are heard. Walter asks Marie-Henriette to flee with him to the world of the sirens, to their underground realms—far from the influence of those who would destroy their love. Marie-

Henriette first refuses. She does not believe in the existence of sirens. But Walter knows better: "They are beautiful and sing to entertain the traveler from the depths of the sea . . ." (p. 176).

Sirens, undines, and Loreleis have existed in legends since time immemorial. These destructive creatures of the sea lured navigators to their island retreats through the hypnotic effect of their melodious songs, and in their lairs their victims drowned. Ulysses had encountered sirens but, being wise, filled his ears with wax so as not to hear these enchantresses and had himself tied to a mast; thus he did not come under their power. Fish-women are cold, calculating hetaera types and are death-dealing. In ancient Egypt, it was said that sirens (who resembled birds) stole the hearts of the dead and of those who had not fulfilled their destinies. They were devouring vampires. In France siren myths were recounted under the name of Mélusine. Psychologically, sirens represent anima figures: unconscious feminine images that are both fascinating and terrifying. If overly obsessed by them, such anima images become destructive and pervert the imagination. Sirens symbolize dream objects, unrealizable illusory passions. They impede the evolution of the ego by depicting perfection in some deceptive retreat, by preventing individuals from struggling through life to develop and learn to cope with tensions. The songs of the sirens captivate the listener who falls under their sway and become victimized by this primitive aspect of life. Whenever a man—or a couple—becomes dominated by a siren, it indicates bewitchment that will terminate in early death.

Walter listens to the call of the sirens. There is one siren in particular who swims toward him and dazzles him by her beauty. It is then that he realizes he wants Marie-Henriette to join him in his new world of perfection. At first, Marie-Henriette is captivated by his description of this imaginary land and of the voice they will take together. Then she becomes frightened. "There are no sirens!" she repeats categorically (p. 177). Walter accuses her of lying and of refusing him. He begs her to follow him into oblivion. She asks him to be patient; she feels too young to die. Perhaps one day she will have the courage to join him. "How am I to live?" he questions. "Oh! I would like to live just once so totally that I would no longer have to love each day" (p. 178). Marie-Henriette pleads with him to

live but a little longer; however, Walter is adamant. He must efface
the pain of life: "I'll show you the place I have chosen. The water is
not deep there" (p. 179).

As Walter listens attentively to the voices of the sirens, which mount
in their urgency, Marie-Henriette becomes moved by their spell
too, and is terrified as she experiences her powerlessness. She sees
Walter's shadow grow larger, spreading blackness all about her. It is
a portent of what is to come.

Walter, your shadow is so black . . . and so long. Oh! so long! It reaches to
the last house . . . Yes, yes, you want to throw yourself into the water; it
will engulf you! (p. 194).

As the water image grows more and more captivating, her senses are
numbed; her rational principle is congealed: "Sometimes the sea
resembles cold marble . . ." (p. 194). Marie-Henriette sings lov-
ingly to the water below. Its spray intermingles with her breath.
She views it now as a cleansing and purifying force. Again she hears
the sirens' voices in the distance, now in contrapuntal rhythms: "To
the sea! To the sea!" (p. 195). As in Beckett's *Happy Days*, where
the continuously encroaching sand finally paralyzes the protagonist,
the water in *The Puerile Lovers* rises and lulls Marie-Henriette and
Walter to their death. Tensions increase as the distinct impression is
given that the entire stage is being flooded with water. The climax
approaches and a commanding voice is heard: "Hurry, hurry, hurry,
faster" (p. 199). From some remote area other voices tell of cosmic
events occurring at this particular moment: stars are falling into the
waters, each engulfed by an implacable but gentle force as life is
being wiped out.

Marie-Henriette's voice takes on the timber of lamentation, a
supplication as she begs for respite. She has grown sleepy; the
struggle against the all-powerful waters of her unconscious is too
much for her. Her strength has ebbed, yet she persists in asking
Walter for one more night on earth—one night of love. However,
the voices, now implacable, compel her toward them in a complex of
rhythmic devices.

In order for rivers to know all things, they altered their course daily . . .
(these are the words, I recall) . . . and as their waters remembered, only by
watching them flow through the grass . . . Are you asleep? . . . one could
learn about all the marvels of the world (p. 200).

Marie-Henriette recalls Walter's words and his need of her. She
sees a ship pass. Fog invades the scene and flashes of lightning are
visible. She has a premonitory vision: she sees a girl drowning. The
sirens' songs grow increasingly imperious. Marie-Henriette consults
l'Etrangère, who encourages her to surrender to Walter: "He is
calling to you in a low voice; yet someone has heard him and he is
ashamed!" (p. 210). Marie-Henriette's desire to merge with universal forces heightens. "Go, go, lift up your skirts and dance barefoot
on the foam," suggests l'Etrangère (p. 211). As Marie-Henriette
leaves, silence and darkness invade the proscenium.

The symbols of water, mirror, and moon merge. The feminine
components prevail over the masculine spiritual forces. The mirror
reflects the physical beings and focuses upon the water it incorporates; the moon, hard and unbending, reverberates in the implacable march of the sea image. It is the moon—that most powerful of
cosmic forces that brings rain, dominates ideas, and activates the
inner world of the protagonists—that also concludes the play. Walter's and Marie-Henriette's death does not come as a surprise. It is a
natural conclusion to the physical and psychological dismember-
ment that has taken increasing hold of the personalities since the
beginning of the drama.

V   *The Mise-en-Scène: Gaston Baty*

Gaston Baty, later a member of the famous French cartel of direc-
tors that included Charles Dullin, Georges Pitoëff, and Louis
Jouvet, was asked by Firmin Gémier to direct *The Puerile Lovers*.
The selection was perfect.

For Baty the theater was more than an intellectual exercise. It
was to pave the way for a numinous experience. When he directed a
play he sought to impose both a spiritual and visceral impact upon
the stage happenings through visual and verbal means. He believed

a *mise-en-scène* should reflect the essence and backbone of a play. It should render palpable in sculptured stage effects the imagery implicit in the dialogue and the sensations that the play arouses. Reinhart, who was Baty's master, used on the stage "architectural forms existing in space." Baty injected mass movement into his sets, along with a dramatic interplay of lights, stylized gestures, and music that circulated throughout the spatial areas. Baty's goal in the theater was a composite of hierarchical elements.

The scenic image—decor, costumes, attitudes, lights—is there to represent what words cannot express, nor music. If it happens that words can say everything, then decors are useless, and each time it becomes indispensable, it must disappear.

To stage a play first means to realize the text; to translate it into plastic and auditive form.[2]

Baty's aim was to arouse and move audiences. It was a titanic endeavor. He sought to draw spectators into a drama's mystery. Words, he felt, were not the only method in which a dramatist could express himself. Words alone were too rational, too limited. For Baty, a deeply religious man, the cosmic and supernatural order had to come into play. In his production of *The Puerile Lovers*, *The Dibbuk* (1928), and *Faust* (1937), he increased the anguish and terror in certain dream sequences through a series of "synthetic visions." He created a unified whole as though he had decanted into one goblet the disparate elements implicit in the theater. The staging of *The Puerile Lovers* suggested mystery and brought into existence two powerfully antithetical worlds: the rational and the irrational, earth and heaven, dream and reality.

Under Baty's aegis *The Puerile Lovers* became a cosmic event. Universal harmonies were expressed by encroaching sensations, rising tides, the fullness of the moonbeams, pervading darkness, and the intrusion of supernatural elements. Man, as viewed in Baty's stage design, became the plaything of his inner world. He was lost in a realm beyond the visible, a victim of his own sensations and longings. Because of his emphasis on the visual aspects of the theatrical endeavor, Baty was accused of deforming the text, of attacking

"Sire le Mot." To this reproach, he replied: "The text has always been an essential part of drama, it cannot say everything." The play "reaches a certain point where the word itself must go. Beyond that another zone begins, a zone of mystery, of silence, which one labels atmosphere, ambiance, climate, whatever you wish. The director's task is to express this realm."[3]

The Puerile Lovers is theater of cruelty. It is a play that unmasks truth. Illusions are allowed to ripen but only when juxtaposed with reality. In this case, beauty with ugliness, youth with decrepitude. Flesh is derided, pride is shattered, the dream scorched. The climate Crommelynck creates in *The Puerile Lovers* is intolerable. Audiences viewing the old Cazou—rejected, solitary, abandoned like an old dog—laugh at this human wreck with its exaggerated gestures. They are also filled with an excoriating *malaise* when identification takes place. Elisabeth is to be pitied. Her inability to accept nature's course turns her into a grotesque figure. More important and more dangerous, however, is her influence on Marie-Henriette. In this instance, she takes on the stature of a murderess: she encourages Marie-Henriette to suicide.

Crommelynck's theater-world is blind and abrasive. Pierre Macabru described *The Puerile Lovers* as "undomesticated theater" and as "rebellious drama," reminiscent in its harshness and brutality of Claudel at his best.[4]

CHAPTER 5

Golden Tripe: *The Miser's Feast* *(1925)*

C ERTAIN plays are born to the wrong times. *Golden Tripe* was one of these. It opened on April 29, 1925, at the Comédie des Champs-Elysées. Director Louis Jouvet had been warned about the certain failure of his project by André Antoine, the founder of the Théâtre Libre. He had told Jouvet that when a play's central theme revolves around money, it "rarely makes money." Even Molière's *The Miser* was performed only eighteen times during the dramatist's lifetime. Antoine's words were prophetic. There were more ushers than there were spectators in the theater during the five evenings *Golden Tripe* played, thirteen people in all on one occasion: nine in the orchestra and four in the balcony.[1]

It is no wonder that *Golden Tripe* failed. How could spectators see themselves as the bone-hard individuals Crommelynck made them out to be? The unicentered characters featured in this play mirror a prevailing *Zeitgeist* which is made up of either callous individuals who react to nothing or of types who have built such defenses against suffereing as to have divested themselves completely of their feeling principle. The slapstick technique in *Golden Tripe*—insults, cruelties, assaults—provokes no human response from the protagonists. Like a series of German expressionist woodblocks, Crommelynck's characters reveal the degenerate nature of the fragmented and faceless beings inhabiting contemporary society. His characters are endowed with the ferocity of Jarry's *King Ubu*. They are wooden, puppetlike, and veer suddenly from one mood to another—from painful frenzy to boisterous gayety. The verbal and physical pyrotechnics of the protagonists as they wobble, grovel, and grope about the proscenium cut through a network of isomorphic relationships by caricaturizing the absurdity of the peregrinations involved. A double action inhabits the stage: the construction and destruction of the human being via the vehicle of laughter.

I *The Plot*

Golden Tripe takes place in a large communal room in a country dwelling. An atmosphere of rustic luxury prevails: highly polished oak furniture decorates the room and attractive dishes line the sideboard.

Relatives, peasants, and servants fill the stage as Pierre-Auguste Hormidas is brought lifeless into his home. The reading of old man Hormidas's will and the shock of inheriting 200,000 francs in gold had overwhelmed him. Onstage the crowd makes merry at the thought of Pierre-Auguste's demise, for they will now become the inheritors of a great fortune. One heir, Froumence, with a pang of conscience, suggests a doctor be called. But Melina, another who will become rich after Pierre-Auguste's death, vetoes the idea. The village doctor is on a house call, she claims with uncontrollable joy, "That's fate!"

Pierre-Auguste is of course not dead, simply in shock. Barbulesque, the veterinarian, is asked to intervene. He suggests that a rereading of the will would be an effective cure. Muscar, Pierre-Auguste's servant, begins the reading. When giggles and then outright laughter emerge from the inert body, paroxysms of anger are heard from the inheritors. However, as soon as his titters cease and Pierre-Auguste slumps back into silence, the inheritors' hopes revive, as well as their gaiety. But jubilation ceases again when Pierre-Auguste begins to smirk, then talks incoherently, and finally rants about his great love, Azelle, who turns out to be none other than a personification of his gold. In his semi-delirium, Pierre-Auguste orders Muscar to fetch Azelle at the inn where he claims she is staying.

In an extraordinary drunken frenzy Muscar takes out his whip and knife and reenacts in Don Quixote fashion his unsuccessful quest for Azelle at the inn. Froumence, Muscar's wife, enters and quickly disarms him. Six girls come onstage. According to the terms of

Hormidas's will, they have been promised upon their marriage the equivalent in gold of a grown cow, providing they are still virgins. In subtle tones Pierre-Auguste demands proof of their virginity. Meanwhile, a Poor Man (we later learn he is the director of the Flying-Theater, an acting company that Pierre-Auguste subsidizes) has made his way onstage and asks for money. A clown begins mimicking the entire interlude: the hypocrisy expressed by the giver, Pierre-Auguste, and the unctuous way of the receiver, the Poor Man. Barbulesque meanwhile has diagnosed Pierre-Auguste's illness as gold sickness and suggests that the only effective medication would be to eat gold. The act ends as Pierre-Auguste mixes his gold (now in dust particles) with dog mess and eats the mixture.

The stage, in semidarkness, reveals Pierre-Auguste in the throws of acute stomach cramps; he has held the gold inside of him for a full month. Shadows become visible on the stage. People with knives lunge at Pierre-Auguste. He is aware of the attempts made upon his life by relatives. Then lights flood the proscenium and the scene has changed: the protagonists are now dressed in seventeenth-century costumes as though enacting roles in the Flying-Theater. Pierre-Auguste is Louis XIV, the Sun or Gold King. When the virgins walk in, he decides to marry the ugliest of them all, Herminie. He looks at her lustfully. Together they will procreate gold. Barbulesque informs him that if he does not evacuate, he will die. "Isn't there another cure for me that will not require me to give up my money?" questions Pierre-Auguste. Annoyed by the naïveté of the request, Barbulesque orders an enema, prunes, and a purge. While Barbulesque prepares his concoctions on one side of the stage, Pierre-Auguste is dialoguing with Herminie on the other in narcissistic nonsense. Herminie (who resembles Alice in Wonderland, in her vicious, terrorizing, and provocative role) looks forward to her union with Pierre-Auguste. Barbulesque observes Pierre-Auguste's blend of agonizing cramps and libidinous looks and orders a potty-chair. Pierre-Auguste is seated, his legs covered with a blanket. Then peasants and inheritors sing out their prayers and good wishes to the newlyweds as the marriage contract is signed. Froumance, hoping that Pierre-Auguste will succumb to a belly laugh and thus expel his gold, takes a whip and beats Muscar while castigating him for his lying and drunkenness. Identifying with the aggressor (or the victim), as do the others onstage, Pierre-Auguste seated on his throne-pot laughs himself to death. The inheritors win the day. Humor—the great liberator—has freed the gold and killed the one who would be its eternal possessor.

II   *The Theme of* The Miser

Despite the fact that, according to André Antoine the theme of avarice is generally unpopular in the theater, it was nevertheless treated with felicity by Plautus, Jonson, Molière, Ghelderode, and others. *Golden Tripe* measures up to *Aulularia* (194 B.C.), *Volpone* (1606), *The Miser* (1668), and *Red Magic* (1931), and in some ways even surpasses them—perhaps through Crommelynck's propensity for crudeness and for the grotesque nature of the situations dramatized.

Whereas Euclio, Plautus's miser in *Aulularia,* is good-humored and his stage concoctions are replete with gags, puns, and confusion resulting from a variety of tricks played on unsuspecting individuals with only occasional touches of pathos, Pierre-Auguste yields to his blindness. He is tyrannized by an obsession that finally becomes a deep-rooted insufficiency, a sickness. At first a bumptious clown who is eaten up by an *idée fixe,* he thrashes about the stage in the drollest of ways. Soon, however, his utter loneliness becomes clearly defined. Plautus's main concern was to amuse the populace and earn money for himself, and he succeeded in his goals. He provoked laughter by the vivacity of the activities introduced on the stage, the exuberance of language and gesture, and by the banter and playful jocularity implicit in the spectacle. *Golden Tripe* inplants itself more deeply into the spectator's psyche. To be sure, Crommelynck's work provokes guffaws and there are few didactic or moralistic attempts interwoven in the situations or dialogue, yet the entire work is peppered with a deep-seated anger, an irony that injects a twinge of *malaise* into the mirth onstage.

Like Ben Jonson's *Volpone,* which was subtitled with reason *The Fox, Golden Tripe* seeks to ridicule, expose, and shame the man obsessed with gold. Both Jonson and Crommelynck attempted to debase this kind of creature, to render him perverse and thus

ludicrous. Volpone, a Venetian miser, feigns his own death in order
to dupe his grasping heirs, and is helped in this masquerade by his
servant Mosca; cruelty battles cruelty. Moreover, Jonson not only
observes the salient characteristics of the miser, as had Crommelynck, but depicted in detail the slow absorption of a personality
by this monomania. The satire created by Jonson and Crommelynck
owes a debt to medieval tradition: the keenness of perception and
the uninhibited manner in which Volpone and Pierre-Auguste play
with people, objectify them, and use them to suit their own needs.

Molière's miser, Harpagon, amasses gold for the pleasure it will
offer him, or so he thinks. Gold is a guarantee against old age,
impotence, and death. For Harpagon, then, gold becomes a vehicle
for a type of Faustian renewal and gratification of lustful desires. His
avarice has so perverted him that it becomes the motivating force for
all of his acts and the cause for his own dishonesty, as well as that of
his children and servants. Such devices are omitted in Crommelynck's work. His characters are relatively simple: hysterical,
blundering, crude, and naïve. They are obsessed with only one
degree of lunacy and would resort to murder to achieve their ends.
In Harpagon's case, as long as his complex is fed, as long as it
dominates his pattern of existence, all continues on its regular
course. However, when he yields to his sensual impulses, when he
decides the world is his and the demoniacal power urge takes hold of
him, his realm disintegrates. His money vanishes and his plans to
marry a young girl are dispelled. Yet despite his cruelty, Harpagon
has children who love him and seek his love in return. Pierre-
Auguste, on the other hand, functions alone in a realm divested of
love. In his fantasy world he conjures up an *anima* figure, Azelle,
who symbolizes gold. Since he cannot relate to real women, his
pitiful personality is far more tragic than Harpagon's.

Hieronymus, Michel de Ghelderode's miser in *Red Magic*, underscores the dangers involved when breaking out of a single-track
existence. Hieronymus seeks to reproduce gold as does Pierre-
Auguste. But whereas Crommelynck's protagonist eats the substance, Hieronymus allows his virgin wife together with a young
man—handsome and virile—an alchemist, to produce their concoctions. He is tricked by the young pair into believing that the wife has

actually given birth to gold and goes to the brothel to celebrate this blessed event. Upon his return he is blamed for two murders that have occurred in his home and is punished for them. In Ghelderode's realm the infernal regions depicted are no longer the jocular worlds filled with puns, jokes, and banter of a Plautus, Jonson, or Molière, or even Crommelynck; but rather, it is the sinister universe replete with demoniacal forces where individuals are benumbed with hatred and vice runs rampant. Comedy has been banished; cruelty of the basest kind reigns supreme.

III *The Psychology of the Miser*

What is the etiology of the miser that dramatists have been inspired to endow this type with life? What is Crommelynck's etiology in particular?

In a well-adjusted and relatively "normal" person, the ego (the center of consciousness) is made up of many complexes, of "a whole mass of ideas pertaining to the ego." The ego-complex, as it is called, is not only able to cope with most problems relating to the individual, but also finds direction to "associations and ideas." When a person is deeply disturbed, however, the psychic totality may become fragmented and split up into various complexes. Pierre-Auguste is a classic example of this kind of fragmentation. He may be said to be suffering from an obsession or a complex.[2]

When such split-offs do occur, each complex may be looked upon as a kind of "miniature self-contained psyche which . . . develops a peculiar fantasy life of its own."[3] When and if a complex should become virtually autonomous, as is the case with Pierre-Auguste, the resulting fantasies assume abnormal proportions; they become a kind of "vassal" no longer willing to give "unqualified allegiance" to the suzerain.[4] When Pierre-Auguste is brought onstage in a semicomatose state, he emerges from it with giggles followed by paroxysmal laughter, then coprophilia, as though he were suspended midway between illusion and reality. While he is awake, his fantasies pursue their course and are expressed in his actions and attitudes.

Complexes have a kind of electric current: they release emotional charges and feeling tones. When exceptionally deep-rooted complexes break through into consciousness, they may erupt with such violence that they invade the entire psyche, thus acting physically upon the person, as shown by Pierre-Auguste's reaction to the will-reading ceremony before the beginning of the play. He was so stunned, he lost consciousness. The power of the complex had altered his respiration, blood pressure, and circulatory system.

What is the destiny of a person who becomes dominated by a complex? As the complex inflates, it grows like a cancer and its energy bombards rational attitudes and thought processes, making such an imbalanced individual a perfect target for the satirist or dramatist. As Pierre-Auguste's complex increases in dynamism, everything he does, thinks, and feels (if he is capable of feeling at all) is centered on it. Distorted notions, words, places, and associations are evoked by this one interest. The imbalance and exaggeration that ensue are sculptured by Crommelynck in his atrophied protagonist. The sudden changes of mood during the course of the play, for example, embody Pierre-Auguste's highly violatile personality. When a subject or situation facing him does not relate in some way to his complex, it is rejected; whereas relatively insignificant statements or acts he feels are associated with his complex become all-important. Pierre-Auguste's sudden rages, his lyric tirades, pettiness, and his obstinacy are explicable and are part of an overall picture. A word, a glance, a raised finger, a tilt of the head may elicit a burst of anger or tears—a violent reaction that is always out of proportion to the situation. Such antics occur countless times in *Golden Tripe*: when Pierre-Auguste delights over his gold and is angered at having given six bags of it away on the spur of the moment; when he extends alms to the director of the Flying-Theater, then suddenly feels threatened in his own generosity. Assuming pathological portions, his reactions eventually lead to his demise.

Pierre-Auguste's emotionally chaotic state prevents him from thinking clearly. This inner confusion is admirably depicted by Crommelynck in the protagonist's disconnected dialogue and perpetual activity; in the irrational sequences of events reminiscent of a series of light motifs jumbled together without rhyme or reason. The greater Pierre-Auguste's thought deprivation, the more intense is his confusion of speech, repetitiousness of language, and meaninglessness of reactions. The verbigerations manifested in the half-sentences and semiphrases flung about and Pierre-Auguste's sluggish thought processes, or what might be termed his *engourdissement mental*, is fertile terrain for Crommelynck the satirist and humorist.

IV   *The Symbology of Gold*

Why is gold so prized that its possession should be the life-goal of so many throughout the centuries?

Gold has been equated with the highest and purest of human values: *aurum*, a spiritual, intellectual, and solar force. For the alchemist, gold represented the fourth state, the fruit of spirit and supreme illumination, the final processes in the creation of the philosopher's stone. Its values are therefore positive when experienced in harmony with the soul; but negative, as in any force, when it usurps the life principle, when it leads to the scorching of one's being.

The Midas myth serves as an excellent example of a man overwhelmed with a desire for this precious metal. Midas asked Bacchus, who had promised to give him what his heart desired, the following:

> "Give me," says he (nor thought he ask'd too much),
> That with my body whatsoe'er I touch,
> changed from the nature which it held of old,
> May be converted into yellow gold." [Ovid]

Midas was unaware of the extremes to which such a gift could lead. When everything he touched, even food and drink, was transformed into gold, he realized he was starving in the midst of his great wealth and was growing steadily weaker. His distress was so acute that he implored Bacchus to take back his gift, which had become a curse. Bacchus ordered Midas to bathe in the Pactolus River, which would cleanse him of his previous desires. Archetypal in nature, myths emanate from man's most primitive depths and as such have universal and eternal significance.

Pierre-Auguste is a twentieth-century Midas who has no Bacchus to restore his balance. His life is a paradigm of the word used to describe his obsession: *miser*, which comes from the French word *misère* ("wretched"), whose Latin root *avarus* means "greedy" and "avid." Misers are engulfed in their own inner whirlwind, in their own "maw," and rarely if ever have the will or ability needed to emerge. Given the gold, it becomes the focal point of Pierre-Auguste's existence; it displaces the Eros principle—human love. For example, when he calls for his Azelle, the audience is at first disconcerted and believes her to be a corporeal figure, then realizes that his rapturous love lyrics are addressed to humanized gold.

> She sat down, sad, resigned. She awaited a smile.
> "Azelle, when I will have a twenty-franc piece, round
> and without debt, I will buy you white gloves and a
> bouquet of spring flowers."
>   Is it an illusion? No! Let us say that it's an
> Azelle of gold (p. 33).

Confusion grows in Pierre-Auguste's mind between his personal gold, Azelle, for which he has worked so hard, and the gold he inherited with ease, a collective entity. The trauma is so intense, it shows the extent of his monomania. He screams out his terror in short pants:

Mine? Where are mine? Here; Azelle everywhere, Azelle nowhere! . . . Or else the vile metal has changed into gold via contact with my precious savings . . . Or else gold has no soul, no personality, no surname. Gold has no tears, no smile. It is gold, a great quantity of gold! Neither Carolus, nor Louis, nor Napoleon, nor Azelles! (p. 41).

His mental perturbation is so acute that the repetition of "gold," "mine," and "thine" in rhythmic interludes indicates the humor involved in his loss of identity.

Interesting also is the name Azelle. The first two letters *a* and *z* may be associated with the alchemist's azoth (quicksilver) or the alpha and omega of the transformatory property that Paracelsus had equated with universal remedy. This chemical substance was extremely important to both the scientific alchemist and the charlatan goldmaker, which is, symbolically, what Pierre-August seeks to become.

What transmutations! Let's place it close together. It combines, more so than saltpeter or sulfur, a terrifying explosive force. A glance, unfortunately placed, may inflate it and the house shatters with a burst of thunder (p. 34).

The alchemist personified their inert chemical and metallic entities; similarly Pierre-Auguste's gold takes on the form and contour of a woman. Moreover, both he and some alchemists were convinced that gold could be created and procreated. As Pierre-Auguste states: "I will place my money, which will then procreate" (p. 80). His reason for marrying Herminie, the virgin of his choice, is to pursue the gestation process: the gold within him will fructify the feminine principle.

That Pierre-Auguste eats his gold is also perfectly in order. Masticating, swallowing, and digesting are activities that require the taking in of outside substance so as to perpetuate life's forces—a *renovatio*. Pierre-Auguste assimilates gold; thus it becomes a kind of hierophany.

When Pierre-Auguste blends the gold dust with dog mess and then eats it, his act becomes meaningful to the humorist as well as to the psychologist. Among primitive peoples, excrement is filled with a "mana-charge" and whatever emerges from the body is considered a creative, fructifying, and potent force. On the stage, however, such an act is so repugnant and so improper as to embarrass the spectator; thus it enters into the domain of comedy. According to Freudian dictum, the spectator's inhibitions are removed and the pleasure principle is released. Laughter inevitably ensues with this kind of *regressus ad uterum*.

Pierre-Auguste must die because he has reached a state of mental and physical deterioration beyond recovery. The mastication of gold and dog mess has not led to renewal but rather to stagnation. Had he not imprisoned the precious metal within him, he might, symbolically at least, have broadened his vision and life experience. Death, therefore, is the only possible conclusion; masterfully handled on the stage, it becomes the carnival's finale.

V *Onomastics*

It is in the variety of his comic techniques that Crommelynck proves his mastership in the theatrical field. Like Rabelais and Jarry, he uses onomastics (the meanings and associations implicit in names) as a vehicle for comedy. Scatological allusions, grotesque interferences, and representations of the protagonists' salient characteristics prevail in the names.

The valet *Muscar* is a liar, drunk, hypocrite, and wife-beater. His name may be associated with muscatel wine and thus indicates his propensity for alcohol. In his stupors Muscar handles a whip and knife with expertise, revealing his hostility toward his employer and the world at large. In that Muscar may also be linked to deer musk, a strong-smelling substance obtained from the sac under the skin of the abdomen of a male deer, the name implies an odoriferous—and to some repugnant—quality. In addition to these allusions, the name resembles that of Mosca, Volpone's valet who is unctuous and servile. Muscar, then, incorporates a panoply of traits, including those of his master, tangible during sequences of extreme hyperactivity when his choleric nature emerges in all of its bitterness. As his name indicates, Muscar is a Dionysian individual; thus there is nothing rational about him as he prances, dances, pivots about, acts the clown, thrusts his hands forward when angered, withdraws them when corroded with fear, or snivels with cowardice. Therefore, when Barbulesque asks Muscar, "Now think. Think. And think, now" (p. 21), the humor of the scene is pronounced. Barbulesque is asking him to act antithetically to his nature. To insist that a drunk or a volatile and irascible human being think logically, that he proceed "regularly" and "slowly" when his entire being functions spasmodically as in a series of tremulous vibrations, is to impose Cartesian logic on a hysteric or placing a lid on a bubbling volcano.

The name Froumence recalls the French verb *frouer* ("to pipe"), used as a decoy in bird catching. Such is the role Froumence plays in *Golden Tripe*: a ploy whose screech attracts her prey, Pierre-

Auguste; whose ways tantalize and at times even subjugate him. Pierre-Auguste likes her outspoken nature and considers her his friend. At other instances he suspects that this sensual and passionate female and her husband, Muscar, are intent upon possessing his gold and that their acts masquerade their real intentions.

Barbulesque, the veterinarian, is a descendant of King Ubu. Gross and vulgar, he is probably the only one in the drama who speaks to the point and acts authentically. As his name indicates, he is the direct outgrowth of burlesque comedy: the word *burlesque* is derived from the Italian *burlare* ("to joke"); it implies clowning and caricature of word and gesture. Burlesque is a kind of farcical play replete with exaggeration and raucous as well as provocative language. Moreover, Barbulesque is the only "slightly" humanitarian character in the drama, and this probably because he is surrounded by animals, not humans. Melina mocks his profession, downgrading it at every occasion. She chides him for having offered his services to a human being and claims: "Do you take Pierre-Auguste for a stingy pig that one leads by the nose? or a hen who lays long eggs by placing his head below his rump?" (p. 16).

Proud of his profession, Barbulesque grows annoyed with the derogatory allusions made upon his work and suggests that those present seek "a doctor whom you will call thaumaturge." Muscar immediately distorts the name to "Thomas-Purge," a direct reference to Rabelais' character in *Gargantua and Pantagruel* (Book II), the learned Englishman who knew alchemy, magic, geomancy, astrology, and philosophy. It was with this "vainglorious Englishman" that Rabelais' Panurge argued in sign language, each gentleman placing his hands in the most ludicrous of areas in order to make himself understood. It is with Panurge-style wit, cunning, and punning that Barbulesque orders Pierre-Auguste to take a purge: a combination of *pan* ("all") and *urge*, which when contracted reads *p-urge*.

In drawing Barbulesque in cursive lines, Crommelynck's intention was to deride doctors and medicine as well as women. For example, Barbulesque compares the female to a hen who lays her eggs every nine months rather than every few hours or days, and arouses ire as he places his *bons mots* in the presence of the ladies onstage. In a mock examination of Pierre-Auguste (reminiscent in its explosive hilarity of Jules Romains' "great" Doctor Knock), Barbulesque asks a series of absurd questions in the most serious of manners: "Were you ever asphyxiated?" Or "Did you ever fall into water?" (p. 22). Sganarelle in Molière's *Doctor in Spite of Himself* is a medic forever quoting and misquoting Aristotle's wise words in the most irrelevant of situations; Barbulesque's nonsense is equally amusing, as attested to when he speaks of the evil effect of thoughts on health:

Let us chase the callosity from the imagination and the imagination from the callosity: say your rosary from beginning to end. Are you cured? (p. 20).

Molière's Sganarelle keeps removing and replacing his hat on his head throughout the examination ritual, whereas Pierre-Auguste takes off his shoes, wiggles his toes, counts them, plays with them, even airs them—and all of this on Barbulesque's recommendation because he asserted that Pierre-Auguste's malady originated in his toes.

In keeping with the farcical and ebullient nature of his name, Barbulesque continues his puns throughout the play, such as for Pierre-Auguste's purge; "This Roman purge you wanted to give your parents" will consist of "a dose of oil of mussolin" (p. 104). It is Barbulesque again in true burlesque style who suggests Pierre-Auguste sit on a potty-chair and wait for events to occur.

Three inheritors—*Melina, Frison, Prudent*—are also caricatured in onomastic style. Melina, in which the verb *mêler* ("to mix," "blend") is implicit, is a mixture of all that is possessive, domineering, hurtful, and heartless. She is a kind of *mélinite* (a powerful explosive formed with acid), a volatile and energetic force. Like the dancer at the Moulin Rouge in the late nineteenth century who was dubbed La Mélinite, so Crommelynck's character is a torpedolike human being. Frison ("to curl") bends over backward throughout the play to please, to subvert, to acquire. He literally turns himself into a curl to achieve his end. Prudent is wiser and less eratic than the other two as he attempts to hide his lust for money and present a pseudo-intelligent visage to the audience.

VI *Moods*

Crommelynck used moods as a comic device. They build up or diminish certain humorous interludes through an alteration of atmosphere and rhythms, thus creating inner and outer dynamisms that are then integrated into the play's composition.

When a play begins with a near-death and terminates with a real one, it may at first not appear conducive to jocularity, but the extremes to which the activities are carried emphasize the absurdities involved and thus the humor of the situation. As a result of the dichotomies of mood and atmosphere, the series of harsh silhouettes emerge in forceful brushstrokes and with Daumierlike acerbity.

At the outset of *Golden Tripe,* the mood of anguish is quickly dispelled by jocularity as the inheritors delight over Pierre-Auguste's probable death. Now all obstacles, they believe, that prevent them from acquiring the gold have been removed. With Pierre-Auguste's return to life, a sudden alteration of mood is heralded by a whole series of facial grimaces, ranging from frowning brows to downward glances and tightened lips—as the many interstices punctuating the ribaldry of the inheritors that preceeded only seconds before. The unrestrained joy of children at play returns each time Pierre-Auguste seems to slump into death. Once his hiccupy laughter, chuckles, and repressed giggles impose themselves upon the scene and he is definitely alive, their faces, transformed into livid masks, take on the rictus of gargoyles.

The *diseuse* Yvette Guilbert once wrote that there are over a hundred different ways of smiling. *Golden Tripe* is a paradigm of this dictum. Rarely are audiences made privy to such nuances of laughter; indeed, Pierre-Auguste's return to the world of the living is measured by a virtual orchestration of snickers, titters, and belly laughs. Each tonality is a reflection of his inner architecture, each modulated to suit his mood and physical well-being. The half-suppressed laughter of discomfiture, the giggles and rapid interludes of jubilation revealed in his near disbelief of his good fortune, the grinding screeches and grins, the macabre and monstrous facial contortions accompanying the will-reading ceremony expand the meaning and depth of this kind of character as well as the humor of

the situation. Pierre-Auguste's harmonic and cacophonous emanations expressed in laughter may become for the seasoned actor an
unforgettable vehicle for self-expression and creativity.

The author's attempt to shift the moods with suddenness when
Muscar reads Hormida's will adds to the satire implicit in the legal
language and causes the hilarity of the sequence. The legacy made
to each individual is in keeping with the personality involved. Frison is willed Hormidas' "last sign" and "with it the will to blow up a
pig's bladder which he will hang above his door." Prudent is given
Hormidas's "last thought."Melina receives his potty-chair, "with its
leather pad and its earthenware pot." The burgomaster will acquire
"his body with all that it contains, the lean and the fat, the large and
the fine, the inert and the volatile entities, all his mortal remains
with their appendages." As for Muscar, the gold chain and some
money will be his due. Froumence acquires the deceased's bed.
The young virgins will be given the "equivalent in gold of an adult
cow" upon their marriages. Pierre-Auguste inherits 200,000 francs
in gold to be found in the wall in the chimney. The inheritors
express their reactions in small gasps, staccatolike hiccups and
chuckles, outrageous guffaws, and brusque, nervous, automatic, or
intense giggles—most frequently accompanied by pathological facial
expressions. One is reminded in certain respects of the will-reading
scene in Petronius' *Satyrica*: "All my heirs shall receive their
legacies on condition that they cut up my body and eat it in public.
Let them gulp down my flesh as eagerly as they damned my soul."[6]

So deeply involved is Pierre-Auguste in his own *idée fixe* that he is
unaware of the attitude of those surrounding him. The gap between
his fantasy world and reality will never be breached and is, con-
sequently, humorous in that it points up to ridicule the naïveté of
the monomanic individual. Pierre-Auguste, now near hysteria from
shock, veers from screams to scoldings, from cajoling to ranting.
Like Don Quixote, he has to be "insane" to survive in an atmosphere he has himself created; like Candide or the good soldier
Schweik, he too will be forced to suffer a series of trials.

A hallucinatory mood is ushered in when Pierre-Auguste begins
his tender love lyrics: "Oh! my beautiful, my good, my dear golden

Azelle" (p. 41). The inflated language used by this lanky, puppetlike creature when reciting his words of passion is out of proportion with the sordid nature of his views and the egotism of his entourage, thus underscoring the tragic but also the farcical nature of his rantings. His inability to relate to others, particularly to women, except in an extravagant or outrageously lewd manner, is even more jarring to the prevailing mood created by his tender and poetic lines to Azeile—thus injecting an even more absurd tone into the stage play.

The fact that he is rich makes Pierre-Auguste feel powerful. His authority, therefore, will remain unchallenged, he notes. Once he has accepted that he is a man of wealth, his mood and laughter grow wild, mad, uncontrolled, instinctive, as though all of his inhibitions have been released. He dances and prances about the stage in slapstick routine; his lanky legs, his quixotic gestures, and his bizarre eye movements setting and altering the mood. Merriment grows to such an extent that he seems overwhelmed by his own jubilance. Such moods of mirth are superseded by bouts of anger: in one scene Pierre-Auguste begins throwing vases and anything else upon which he can lay his hands. When Melina accuses him of being mad and demands he be taken to a mental institution, Pierre-Auguste informs her—with all of his wits about him—that the rich are never incarcerated, for they are the ones to wield the power; they are masters, not servants. Were he to destroy his entire house, that would be his prerogative, he asserts with bravado.

When Pierre-Auguste gives the inheritors six bags filled with gold in a moment of delirious generosity, he regrets his act moments later and laughs nervously, then with concern, and finally with anguish. Like an old satyr—half man and half goat—he reveals his cupidity as his giggles grow more raucous. Muscar, caught up in the excitement of the moment, laughs amazedly, then bedazzledly, finally effervescently. To emphasize the cupidity of those involved, Crommelynck has the protagonists repeat the word *take* as each takes his sack of gold. The sequence emerges as a type of liturgical prayer, an incantation ritual to God Mammon. To underscore the religious and thus the collective and eternal nature of man's greed, Melina speaks out in Latin: *"Dominus menor fuit nostris et benedixit nobis*" (p. 38). The alliance of religion and gold provokes laughter among the protagonists—through the shock value of such an association—but it is a fearsome, subdued kind of laughter.

The scenes delineating Pierre-Auguste's lust dispel the somber mood of the gold digger and are therefore particularly titillating. When the virgins first enter, demanding the money promised them upon their marriages, Pierre-Auguste with a smirk demands proof of their virginity. The burgomaster shooes the girls offstage and says: "They are already here, all of them, ready to be milked" (p. 26). The activity comes to a halt; silence is complete. Suddenly the mood is relieved by peals of laughter, described in the text by Crommelynck as "overflowing, warm, palpitating" (p. 27), as the men present salivate at the thought of the deflowering process. Guffaws begin moments later: high-pitched cackling sounds repeated in starts, then trumpeted out with laughter in all tonalities and rhythmic sequences. The stage takes on the grandeur of a kinetic sculpture, of a cacophonous interlude. But as Pierre-Auguste's ways grow more libidinous ogling the virgins, moods of shock set in as he declares in no uncertain terms: "Let the most virgin of them all come forth first," thus ridiculing the entire concept of chastity and by the same token Christ's words, "He that is without sin among you, let him first cast a stone at her" (John 8:8), as well as the parable of the virgins (Matthew, 25). When Pierre-Auguste realizes that should he wed, he might have to give up some of his gold, he pivots around, groans, screams, and claps his hands in anger, to exclaim seconds later in a mood of delirious jubilation: "Money fights its own battles!" (p. 66). Menacing, with jutting jaw, this gawky puppet walks toward the virgins, terrorizing them with his outrageous facial grimaces, his taut brows. Only the ugly Herminie remains. Her name, reminiscent of the ermine that procreates with great ease, attracts Pierre-Auguste. She will be the perfect mate and together they will make gold.

To increase the perturbations, Crommelynck resorts to the theatrical convention of the play-within-the-play technique used with such felicity ever since Corneille's *Comic Illusion*. The play within the play serves to link ideas, situations, and characters, but when used by Crommelynck, it underscores the incongruity of the goings-on. The director of the Flying-Theater first appears as a Poor Man who plays on Pierre-Auguste's generosity. Later, he reveals himself as a theatrical director and depicts the financial plight of those connected with the performing arts on a realistic level, thus disorienting the spectator as well as the protagonist, who no longer knows whether to believe or whether he is deceived. This is a theatrical reality, in that audiences go to the theater for the purpose of being duped, thus entertained. The chasm between the world of illusion and reality, confusion and merriment, pathos and comedy is further enlarged when Pierre-Auguste appears as the Sun King, Louis XIV. The preposterous nature of the situation—the association of seventeenth-century glitter, splendor, and gold, and the spiritual poverty of the protagonists interested only in the material aspect of the purest of metals and in Pierre-Auguste's bodily functions—interweaves a carnival and buffoonlike infrastructure into the happenings. The Poor Man's words spoken in Act II are fitting in Act III: "Ah! you have the most sublime of souls!" (p. 69).

Such noble sentiments are rendered even more grotesque in the last scene. Pierre-Auguste, firmly ensconced on his potty-chair, receives his bride dressed in a magnificent seventeenth-century wedding dress and signs the nuptial agreement. An umbrella placed over Pierre-Auguste's head, symbolizing a type of canopy, isolates the couple from the rest of the entourage. Froumence steps forward and informs them that she has promised a "comedy" and is now ready to keep her word. With dramatic brio Muscar hands her his whip. She begins to use it on him with gusto. In a circular whipping game she reduces him to his knees as the inheritors look on aghast. The caper is taken seriously. Froumence's anger and whipping intensity increase, dizzying those around her. Slowly, Pierre-Auguste's attempt to comprehend the events diminishes; he begins to laugh, at first spasmodically, then with vigor. Muscar begins kissing the bottom of Froumence's skirt and then drags himself before her on his knees. Pierre-Auguste can no longer contain his laughter, nor his intestines. The festivities approach their visceral finale in a paroxysmal interplay of comedy-tragedy: Pierre-Auguste dies, and the inheritors are jubilant at the effectiveness of the sideshow.

VII *Gestures*

Like the mimes of old who used to be considered representatives of collective ideas or feelings, Crommelynck's characters not only use intellectual or verbal means to create humor, but gestures as well to evoke guffaws. Mimetic interludes, visual play of hands, feet, and body stances are exaggerated, minimized, and placed in harmony or in disaccord with the words or situations throughout the drama—mostly aimed at triggering off a mood of hilarity.

Gestures delineate characters by singling them out in terms of a particular phobia. A comparison may be made, for example, between Beckett's Lucky, in *Waiting for Godot,* and Muscar, in the visual impact of their gestures. Lucky's miming scenes, a fitting background for his metaphysical anguish revealed in his irrational talk coupled with his groveling and varied spatial configurations accomplished with his hands and feet, may be opposed to Muscar's drunken and whipping bouts. Like Lucky, Muscar becomes a vessel for emotion. As he hops about creating a mood of levity, he is also expressing his hostility toward authority and mankind in general. His bodily distortions, grimaces, crudeness, and vulgarity are all aimed to shock, disorient, and destroy complacent attitudes. His agitation, sobs, and joys are frequently delineated by the arch of a finger, a raised arm, a sudden twist of the neck or head. As he pivots about his gawky legs, enigmatic smile and frequently abusive language are knit together in a dialectical image, underscoring his dissatisfactions as well as his limitations and pettiness. Pierre-Auguste's rages, vituperations, demonstrative and affective motions, pirouettes, thrusts, lunges, drags, pulls, and feet-stamping episodes are all exteriorizations of an inner scape designed to broaden the scope of the themes involved and to intensify the comic-tragic situation of such beings.

Gestures, like semiotics, have a double impact upon the viewer. They fill his mind with spatial images and also impinge upon the protagonists' privacy. By means of gestures, one's perception grows increasingly more acute and symbols are experienced as tunnels leading to an arcane realm. In Genet's *The Blacks* and *The Screens,* gestures are implicit in the stage language and, as Artaud has declared, are a language in themselves, a kind of hieroglyphics enabling barriers to be pierced and the most secret of thoughts to be deciphered. In *Golden Tripe* the characters reveal their complexities through a highly imaginative counterplay of visual images. Every emotion, wrote Artaud in *The Theatre and its Double,* has its corresponding gesture: anger, joy, lust, exhaustion. The indications concerning the protagonists' bodily movements that Crommelynck has inserted in his text are authentic: each suits the intent of the personalities involved. The manner, gait, and physical participation of the protagonists in the dramatic network as a whole are comparable to a series of rhythmic sequences and kinetic sculptures.

Gestures may be viewed as mechanistic and energetic entities causing friction and increasing an individual's potential. In Ionesco's *The Killer,* the protagonist's role is reduced to a series of bodily movements: shrugging of shoulder, snickering, smirking. In Artaud's *The Cenci* and in Racine's *Bajazet,* mutes gesticulate through the entire scene, instilling an atmosphere of terror in the stage happenings. The whipping sequences in the final scene of *Golden Tripe* create two counterimages as in a two-ring circus: Froumence and Muscar in their rapidly paced circular configuration on one side, Pierre-Auguste immobilized in royal grandeur on his potty-throne on the other.

The introduction of a clown into the stage play serves to quantify the importance of visual modulations. Because of the caricatural manner in which these episodes are handled, the spirit of jocularity is emphasized. When the clown "placidly" imitates Muscar's gestures as well as those of Pierre-Auguste and the Poor Man in Act II, Crommelynck's buffoon is vastly different from Shakespeare's Fool in *King Lear,* who amuses but in whose words wisdom is embedded. Crommelynck's clown is silent. He is also reminiscent of the ancient French, Italian, and English jesters whose function it was to amuse by exteriorizing and aggrandizing certain secret or grotesque situations in a series of visual configurations. It is the raw and ribald antic that Crommelynck's clown expresses and that impresses itself in the mind's eye.

Crommelynck's clown is also a mime, and at certain moments he is reminiscent of Philocleon who, in Aristophanes' *The Wasps,* attempts to get out of the house in which his son has imprisoned him. Standing near the director of the Flying-Theater, the clown imitates the obsequious gestures of the man requesting money. To increase the merriment of this alms-giving ceremony, he mimes the domineering and authoritarian attitude of the dispenser of charity. As if this were not sufficient to create a mood of ribaldry, Muscar takes his place behind the clown and in an orchestration of mirth and delight mimes the gestures of the others in a veritable comedy routine.

Analogies may be drawn between the Italian stock characters of the *commedia dell'arte*, whose goal it was to amuse and ridicule, and Crommelynck's protagonists. Pierre-Auguste is a duplicate of Pantalone, that old Venetian merchant who was forever afraid of losing his gold. Muscar is comparable to the *zannies*, those scoundrel servants who performed the most enchanting but dishonest of deeds. The mélange in *Golden Tripe* of the zanni spirit, anger, and the indignation of a Pantalone set in the sordid atmosphere of a possessive and grasping French peasantry creates an unforgettable spectacle.

Crommelynck arouses spirited banter through repetition of gestures in nonrecognition scenes, thereby paving the way for increased ambiguity, confusion, and misunderstanding between the protagonists, while at the same time entering into complicity with the audience. When, in Act I, the notary suggests he be paid his fee for probating Hormidas's will and the taxes in the settlement of the estate also be paid before Pierre-Auguste disposes of his money, he seems to be talking to a deaf ear. Pierre-Auguste's attention meanwhile has been diverted to his fantasy figure Azelle, and then to the food to be ordered for dinner: rabbits, meats, and leather, eggs from the chicken coops, milk from the stable, and a host of ridiculous requests. All the while, however, Pierre-Auguste keeps repeating that he wants a receipt from the notary for the money he will give him. During the scene the notary keeps handing him the receipt in question, but to no avail. Pierre-Auguste pays no attention to the notary's antics. Finally, out of desperation, the notary loses patience and throws the entire briefcase at Pierre-Auguste, after remonstrating with him for his utter senility: "Are you crippled?" (p. 40).

Rage is expressed by Muscar when he brandishes his knife as had the knights of old their swords. Muscar advances on Pierre-Auguste, the butt of his anger: "Here is Muscar's knife that blazes in the midst of fog . . . Breathe, breathe, your last breath on this blade, which does not retain mist!" (p. 50). Repetition, alliteration, and wild imagery are likewise instrumental in underscoring the humor of this outrageous incident. Muscar's boldness, for example, is such at this juncture that Pierre-Auguste is mortified and remains in a state of virtual terror until Froumence enters accompanied by the six virgins. Muscar's bravura in turn is suddenly dissipated: his obsequious nature emerges with deep bows and a few well-placed *"Requiescat in Pace,"* thus parodying the entire play of moods and personalities (p. 50).

The most agonizing gesture occurs in Act III during Pierre-Auguste's stomach-cramp sequence. The pain he feels is rendered so graphically, like volcanic eruptions noted on a seismograph, that in an attempt to dominate his agony, it forces him to pant, grunt, run, jump, sit, hold his abdomen, and fling his arms about. But his pirouettes are to no avail. At the end he doubles over and falls limply on his throne-chair, only to rise moments later in a series of spasmodic laughing bouts. Indeed, Baudelaire was correct when he asserted that laughter is satanic, that it is the kind of grimace embedded in "ice" that "rends the guts."[6]

The miser as viewed in *Golden Tripe* is a character fit for ridicule; he is also a pathological creature to be pitied—an eternal force in human nature. The ambivalence and provocative nature of the humor Crommelynck underscores in his play, the distortions and unbalanced nature of the characters corroded by a monomanic view of life, stand out throughout the work in sharp relief. Crommelynck has incised his rigid beings in unforgettable mobile images; they breathe and grow and rise in all of their deformed grandeur as they expel life's outrageous cruelties in shrill noises, perplexing grins, and in mad farcical laughter.

CHAPTER 6

Carine *or* The
Young Girl Mad About Her Soul:
From Ingénue to Amazon
(1929)

*C*ARINE is the first of Crommelynck's Boulevard plays. It deals
with themes that are *à la mode*; its theatrical conventions are
obvious; its farcelike aspect is played down.

Produced at the Thâtre de l'Oeuvre under Lugne-Po̎'s direction
on December 19, 1929, *Carine* is an undeservedly neglected play.
Although the themes are not new (Crommelynck dramatizes a world
of perversion and cruelty set against one of purity and tenderness),
the richness and variety of his characters are innovative and range
from refined, delicate, and ethereal to sadomasochistic. Crommelynck's introduction of ballet scenes mimed by masked dominoes
is equally intriguing. These kinetic beings not only enter into the
conflicts enacted onstage during the course of the drama, but also
engender a sense of mystery and terror. Reminiscent of ancient
shadow figures, they not only reenact in their own stylized manner
things past, but are also portents of events to come. Influenced by
the sprightly, fanciful characters in Marivaux's and Musset's dramas,
Crommelynck created his own characters and domino figures. They
bear his particular stamp; their dialogue is dense, savory and expressionistic; the imagery sculpted in bold relief, the love sequences
lyrical.

I *The Plot*

The action of this one-act play takes place in the hall of a large
seventeenth-century castle. Christine and Nency, friends from con-

Carine, or The Young Girl Mad About her Soul   105

vent days, are chatting about Carine and the tricks she used to play
at school. They speak of Carine's love of fun and her recent happy
marriage. A rather uncouth gentleman enters. He bears no proper
name and is alluded to as The Hunter. He makes advances to Nency
who rejects him first, but then with playful laughter enjoys his
caresses.

Carine and Frederic, her husband, walk onstage after the others
have departed. In love, they sing out their tender, perfect, and
ineffable joy. Nothing is more beautiful than their relationship,
nothing more idyllic. Although Carine's bliss knows no limits, there
is something troubling her, a feeling she cannot understand nor
explain. Frederic tries to reassure her.

Carine's mother, a collective figure called The Mother, enters
after Frederic leaves. Her jacket is bloodstained. She and her
friend, M. Brissague have had an accident while horseback riding.
M. Brissague is carried onstage; his anger is full-blown. He curses
The Mother and she retaliates by threatening to whip him if he does
not desist. Carine's Mother confesses the awful truth to her daughter that she has always been in love with M. Brissague; but not
wanting to be a burden to him, she has allowed The Hunter to
support her. Worse still is a promise she has made to M. Brissague.
In order to keep his interest, Carine is to be his at the appropriate
time. The innocent Carine is traumatized by this confession.

The mood changes. Two Dominoes—one in black, the other in
silver—enter the stage wearing masks and long cloaks (as was the
custom in French mime drama and the Italian commedia dell'arte).
As the dominoes glide about the proscenium, they carry a giant red
doll and play out a love game with it, miming the trials and trib-
ulations of ecstatic love as well as those of more sordid pleasures.

Frederic returns. Carine's once beautiful and serene expression
has turned to one of grief and terror. She has suddenly become
revolted by everything sexual and refuses to let Frederic come close
or touch her. Frederic is disconsolate, unable to understand her
sudden change. The Black Domino laughs through his mask at
Frederic's agitation, mocking and deriding him. A Silver Domino
appears wearing the mask of one of Carine's convent friends. She
and her other school chums gossip. They recall her convent pranks

and secrets and relate her statement that "Frederic was not a man"
(p. 87). Frederic is stunned by what he hears. Two Domino couples
enter, embrace, and begin miming the misunderstanding that has
now arisen between the young lovers. A harlequinade ensues.
Carine enters and stands motionless as if dazzled by the brilliant
lights on the proscenium. Tortured, trembling with fear, afraid to
move, she looks desperately for Frederic. She wants to apologize for
her behavior, confess her grief and terror. A Domino wearing Christine's mask bars her way. Christine wants Carine for herself and
reveals her passion. Carine screams and attempts to flee.

Carine dons a mask and coat but removes both when Frederic
enters. She wants him to try to understand her shocked reaction to
her mother's confession and to Christine's behavior. She is revolted
by the flesh. During their conversation, Carine learns of an affair
Frederic had during their engagement. He assures her that it was
nothing, a mere bagatelle. She is deeply hurt by what she considers
a breach of trust and becomes cold and detached.

The Mother enters and asks her daughter's help once again. M.
Brissague has threatened to leave her unless Carine promises to
yield to his desires. Carine finally consents. She writes to Frederic
informing him of her unwillingness to pursue a life that could only
bring despair. As she makes her way to M. Brissague's room, she
suddenly falls dead. When Frederic learns of her demise, he dies as
mysteriously as she did.

II *The Characters*

The characters depicted in *Carine* include the ingenue, the amazon, the lesbian, and the priapic man.

Carine, as her name implies in Italian (*cara*), is dear, pretty, and
sweet. She is naïveté personified, open but childlike. Her personality leads to her undoing. She is the perfect mate for Frederic, whose
name means faith, trust, and fidelity. Carine and Frederic do not
have the strength of character or the experience necessary to fight
the forces that will destroy them and so passively succumb to the
struggles. They are ever victims of situations.

Carine's demeanor is one of the stereotyped child-martyr who is
used by her mother and friends for their own purposes. Bred in an

overly refined, overly spiritual atmosphere, she has never experienced the darker side of human nature. She has not even reached adolescence and is still in the paradisiac and protected state of childhood. She projects only the "perfect" existence about her, the only one she knows. Suddenly she comes to realize that another domain exists, one of corruption and debauchery. Her world of clarity, whiteness, and beauty was a half-realm that caused her to limp through her short existence. She cannot fight back and falls by the wayside.

The Mother is archetypal in stature. She is the pivotal force of the play. Like the collective figure of antiquity, she takes on the power of the Great Mother, the Great Goddess, the symbol of creation and destruction. In Crommelynck's play, The Mother is negative, devouring, and death-dealing; indiscriminate in her feelings, she acts and reacts impulsively. No rational force intervenes, no evaluation is made of the damage she inflicts upon herself and her daughter. She is reminiscent of Heinrich von Kleist's *Penthesilea* (1808) in which the amazon princess passionately in love with Achilles tears him to pieces in a fit of jealousy. Horrified by her act, Penthesilea kills herself. Crommelynck's Mother is comparable to this ancient princess in that no conflict exists between her passion for M. Brissague and her obligations to her daughter. Carine is used merely as a stepping-stone to further her mother's passion. Never once does her daughter's well-being enter her frame of reference. A slave to her desires, as is Penthesilea, The Mother becomes a murderess. When M. Brissague threatens to leave her she attempts to destroy him and herself in a riding accident. When her plan fails, she confesses her thoughts to her daughter, admitting their ugliness. "Love does not enoble," she tells Carine (p. 39). M. Brissague in Carine's presence accuses her Mother of being a whore, a murderess. Carine has never heard her Mother villified before. She realizes now that she is the center and goal of the argument and is stunned by the baseness of the two individuals. She believed that her Mother was a fructifying force in her life. The Mother has some pangs of remorse and attempts to justify her actions to her daughter. "Nothing was premeditated," she claims, "I just went insane" (p. 42). One may question the validity of her excuse and wonder whether insanity is

sufficient to explain the perpetration of her intended crime. The
Mother seeks consolation and forgiveness from Carine, thus revers-
ing the mother-daughter roles.

She will understand me now that she has also succumbed to the tyranny and
baseness of the flesh! If you love me, Carine, you will understand my
abominable need to keep him (p. 43–4).

Although The Mother does not succeed in killing M. Brissague or
herself, she does destroy her daughter. When she asks Carine to
inform M. Brissague of the intention to yield to his passion, The
Mother causes her to experience the most humiliating degradation.
Carine, shocked by the overwhelming sensuality in her Mother's
life, is even more horrified by the fact that her Mother has never
really loved her. Carine had been sent to convent school because
her Mother was jealous of her daughter's beauty and charm. Similar
to Medea who sacrificed her two sons for the excoriating passion-
jealousy she felt for Jason, The Mother destroys the progeny who
posed a threat to her love relationship.

Christine, Carine's convent friend, is mysterious and frightening.
Her haughtiness, coldness, and dark and secretive ways inspire fear.
Christine tells Nency that she took pleasure in reporting Carine's
activities to the convent authorities and to The Mother. She knew
that Carine would be reprimanded when she overstayed the curfew
or gossiped about others. Christine is paradoxical. She is reserved
and controlled, her gestures are brusque, giving the impression that
powerful instinctuality is being held in check. Slowly, her character
emerges. She is jealous of those who surround Carine. Obsessed
with her, Christine is tortured by her passion. Unable to express her
lesbian love except as an informer, she attempts to control her
feelings. Christine, a solitary figure, is to be pitied for her abnormal-
ity. In Diderot's The Nun we are given an equally trenchant charac-
terization of the lesbian type whose scheming and perverse ways
have dominion over her.

Christine in some ways may be labeled an amazon female. Ama-
zons, described in legends in Greece, Asia Minor, Thrace, and
Lemnos, and written about by Virgil, Strabo, and Plutarch, were

militant, martial women. To establish a matriarchal society, these women enacted masculine situations and performed manly deeds. They bred horses, fought battles, and became the heads of families, whereas the men were reduced to a stud position. To distinguish themselves from other females, they indulged in self-mutilation: they burned off their right breast to become better archers and spear throwers.

As an amazon type, Christine is androgynous, hostile, aggressive, destructive, and energetic. She attempts to dissimulate her problem and to hide her misguided sensuality. Her shame turns to rage at her own weakness. Her anger is projected onto the society she seeks to destroy, as well as on the object of her love.[1] Although her passion emerges frequently in an ugly manner (an informer), she rationalizes that her acts are well-meant. Apologizing to Carine for having reported her during their convent days, she takes pleasure in demanding and then provoking Carine's dismay. She wants to be punished and needs Carine's repudiation of her. Her love-hatred for Carine reaches a frenzy in a scene that may be compared in its sadomasochistic dimension to Genet's *The Maids*. The force of Christine's anger and brutality drive her to Carine whose hand she bites.

If you owe your happiness to me, the imprint of my teeth will make you remember it for a longer time than your memory! (p. 165)

Christine is revolted by Carine's love for Frederic. She cannot tolerate hetero-sexuality. "A stranger need only enter the scene and this so-called purity of yours turns into mud! Carine! You are a whore like all the others" (p. 166). Her vindictiveness and her anger likens her to the Maenads of old. She is ready to destroy Carine with a serpent's bite, as the Maenads had annihilated their sons and lovers.

Nency, on the other hand, is a jolly, well-meaning girl for whom pleasure is an important part of the life experience. She enjoys the world, the favors men bestow upon her, and is not shocked by the various men she encounters. Without illusion or ideals, Nency lives every day to the fullest in a type of hedonistic love of life. Accepting the charms of The Hunter, Nency reacts in playful banter. When Frederic describes his brief premarital liaison with her, he sees it as a fun-loving escapade because Nency looks upon it as such. She is not hurt in the course of events; she enjoys what she can and simply accepts her daily activities.

The Hunter is priapic and lives on a strictly instinctual level. There is nothing refined about him, nor is there anything perverse. He represents an archetype: that of sexuality. A hunter in the real sense of the word, he seeks out his mate in symbolical rape experiences. He will not suffer for his woman nor ever inflict bodily pain upon her. He takes Nency on his lap as he would any female, enjoying her coquettishness, and her pseudo-demure ways. He is delighted with love and life.

The Hunter can react to pain, however. When he sees the depth of Carine's despair, he is moved and attempts to educate her in the realities of his world. He wants to bring her down from her spiritual heights, parochial attitudes, and one-sided views. He philosophizes with Carine on the frequently positive side effects of suffering.

It is through moral pain that one begins to understand the depths of the soul, by suffering of the flesh, the frontiers of the body. Without these, you could not exist (p. 63).

The Hunter's attitude is Claudelian to some extent. Claudel believed in the value of moral and physical suffering, frequently to justify his own libidinous acts. Evil, Claudel said, must be overcome to experience God's domain. However, unlike Claudel's martyrs in *Break of Noon* and *The Announcement Made to Mary*, The Hunter never seeks to go beyond earthly pleasures, he speaks only of such possibilities to Carine. The Hunter is content to preach spirituality—but enjoys sensuality. His words are never fully accepted by Carine, for whom suffering means unbearable, unwanted pain.

III   *The Domino Mimes*

Crommelynck's Dominoes, or Harlequins, may be looked upon as embodiments of intuitions and premonitions. They move about the stage like echos, shadows, unrevealed agents, and dreams—figures haunting and engulfing the atmosphere with a sense of mystery and terror.

Crommelynck's concept of the Domino, or mime, may be likened to that of the Greeks. In Diomedes's words:

The mime is an imitation and irreverent (i.e., secular) expression of some dialogue, or the lascivious imitation of indelicate deeds and words.[2]

For the Greek, mime was an imitative art in which satire, humor, and the power of ridicule blended into one. The first time that Crommelynck introduces audiences to the Domino figures they are presented as a masked couple, one in black and the other in silver. They mime the action that has just preceded onstage. They kiss and gambol about, incarnating the joy and delight of newborn love, emotions experienced by Carine and Frederic on their wedding night. Each of the Dominoes walks in a cloud, a dazed euphoria. Then a macabre note is injected into their ebullient ballet, causing them to stop short. Sharp sensations felt by Carine are depicted as the Silver Domino begins screaming for help, then bursts into strident laughter and offers herself to the Black Domino. Taking on the characteristics of Christine, the Silver Domino begs her partner's forgiveness, then insults and attacks him to provoke feelings of rejection. Mimicking Carine once again, the Silver Domino jumps toward her partner and embraces him. Insults and vindictiveness enter into the love sequences. Ambiguity points up the terror, the scandal, and the future destruction of the protagonists.

Besides showing past events, the Dominoes enact forthcoming ones and also ridicule excesses. Both purity and perversion are considered aberrations. Throughout the miming sequences, Christine, The Mother, M. Brissague, Carine, and Frederic become the butt of ridicule. Subservient to their lust or virtue, none is able to evaluate the impact of his ways; each is viewed as a blind puppet wreaking havoc.

In that the Dominoes replicate past activities and intuit future events, they infuse the drama with a sense of eternity and can thus enter another dimension. Time is no longer eschatological. Events are cyclical and endowed with timelessness and are lived many times by a group of human beings. Looked upon as transcendental figures or archetypes, the Dominoes mirror man in his eternal aspects of sexuality and spirituality, good and evil, problems that have provoked the human species since time immemorial. The sense of eternity infused by the Dominoes is also injected into the dialogue; for example, when Carine and Frederic meet after being exposed to the corruptions of existential life, time becomes an inescapable reality.

> Carine: I ask you just to have patience, for only one day . . .
> Frederic: A hundred days!
> Carine: . . . only one night . . .
> Frederic: A hundred nights!
> Carine: Leave me tonight . . .
> Frederic: Months, years, and my death with your eternity! (p. 174)

> Frederic: I left her yesterday, no, this morning—before—
>   hardly an hour ago! one hour!
> The Hunter: You have forgotten time?
> Frederic: Yes, you might say so—that is, my watch (p. 177).

The masks add an element of mystery to the situations and simultaneously instill moods of confusion and chaos. In France in the thirteenth century, masks or painted faces were referred to as "artifices" and were designed to deceive spectators as well as protagonists. The masks worn at the Feast of Fools frequently terrified onlookers so that they ran away screaming. Horrified by the grotesqueness of their form, the masks of misshapen faces ogling the spectators and the horns plus other "devilish" accoutrements were taken for reality.[3] Crommelynck's Dominoes, too, are designed to disorient and frighten and to underscore the agitation of the proceedings. When the Black Domino sees Frederic in a state of anguish, his mask contours laughter and harsh grimaces, accentuating the proximity of terror and the mechanism of laughter as well as the curiosity these emotions engender.

Curiosity dries me up, but pleasure is blended into anguish. Who are you? Don't answer. Let us put off the moment of discovery (p. 182).

For Crommelynck the macabre may be translated into a rictus, the natural nervous reaction to terror and fear. As Frederic watches the Black Domino embrace the Silver Domino, mimicking Carine's ingenuous attitude and progressive despair and his own discomfiture, he is overwhelmed by feelings of confusion and malaise.

It is impossible to understand anything, nothing seems to fit, nothing is meaningful! Spare me your mockeries; you understand, don't you, that it is Carine alone who can make me cry. When we left each other, we were united like two eyes in a single glance. One hour, hardly! Now I find her in the same place where I had left her, but she looks at me now with invincible dread. She screams, she pushes me away, she flees, she shuts her door! Am I insane? Is she crazy? I don't understand a thing anymore (p. 183).

The masks worn by the two Dominoes are symbols of alienation. They replicate the disjointed worlds in which the protagonists live. Like the masks worn by the primitives during their tribal dances and religious ceremonies, the Black and Silver Dominoes stand for elemental experiences, the transpersonal realm and the *persona* that the rational principle imposes upon individuals. When the Dominoes intervene in stage events, they underscore the chaos, fear, and trembling corroding the hearts of the protagonists. When Carine searches desperately for Frederic, she is barred access to him by the Silver mask. One of the Dominoes, dressed as Christine, tells Carine that she has bitten herself ten times as punishment for the cruelty inflicted upon her beloved: "This single drop of blood, the taste of which is still in my mouth, is like honey to my heart that longs for you" (190). Carine must fight against the Dominoes—who here represent oppressive, evil forces—to reach Frederic.

Crommelynck uses the mask as Genet has in *The Screen*, as a totem, a sign, a cult object of something to be preserved or destroyed. It is not necessarily used as a representative of character, but rather as an exaggeration of collective characteristics. The Black and Silver Dominoes introduce audiences into a fantasy world where unconscious sensations and abstract forces spread turmoil. While searching for Frederic, Carine feels one of the Dominoes breathing down her back and she tries to run, but he jumps in front of her, forcing her toward the stairs.

Accompany me into the only real world of faceless beings. No more brains, no superfluous names! Good-bye worries, mental torment, waiting or vain searches! Put on your mask. Come to the park, enter into the game of our species! . . . Are you afraid? (p. 192).

As a crowd of masked couples floods the stage, Carine becomes a prisoner of these unconscious agents, these supernatural forces that block her happiness. Both outer and inner worlds now become united in their negative atmospheres.

On the other hand, a mood of frolic is injected into the stage events by the Dominoes. As in the Lupercalian and fertility rites dedicated to Faunus in ancient Rome, and replaced in Christian times by festivals honoring the Virgin Mary,[4] so Crommelynck introduces the satyr in the form of the Black Domino. He tells the Silver Domino:

Since I surprised you lying down in the middle of the reeds, I have been haunted by your beautiful legs, which extend like an avenue without end! What a pursuit this afternoon. You bore under your skirt a heaven, and my glance, is its prisoner! (p. 186).

In this instance the Dominoes represent earth principles. They could be dressed in any century French, Italian, or English garments, as aristocrats or as peasants, and remain Dionysian in spirit and phallus worshippers.

The colors worn by the Dominoes are significant, indicating contrasting moods and destinies. The male Domino is black, a color often symbolizing negative, shadowy, infernal characteristics and either an absence or synthesis of all colors. The Black Domino may be said to represent undifferentiated primordial depths. He absorbs light as he does the events and characters in the play.[5] The Black Domino is juxtaposed to the silvery glitter of the feminine Domino, who symbolizes the transformatory value in nature. The alchemist, the romantic, and the man of religion have compared silver to purity, light, crystal, water, the mirror, and the sparkle of diamonds. It is less blatant and forceful than the sun, more subdued, more subtle. It represents the nuances of emotion, those hidden qualities that may be sensed and felt, if not understood. "I am a Domino among others," (p. 167), the Silver Domino states. She is representative of negative and positive values, cupidity and the misfortunes provoked by such a characteristic. The Black Domino is not deceived by her beauty: "Your looks swarm with sin" (p. 167). He calls her a "prostitute." Her egotism and lust are frequently interspersed with tenderness when underscoring the beauties of love as enacted in Carine's plight.

The Dominoes intervene in the stage happenings as protagonists. When playing the part of catalyzing agents, they usher in new situations and emotions. When the Black Domino imitates Frederic, Carine rushes toward him, thinking he is her husband. But she realizes the deception and walks hurriedly in panic as if haunted by some terrible omen. Attempting to increase Carine's fear, the Black Domino tries to ingratiate himself and finally persuades her to don a mask. Carine, terrified by the Domino's brusk ways and his insinuating and carnal gestures, is afraid of the unknown he represents. She seeks desperately to return to her circumscribed, safe childlike realm, the one she had with Frederic and before her marriage. But the Domino will not let her.

You must see that! In the shadow, more mobile than water, only bodies without heads, only blind bodies searching for each other, apprehending each other with an instinct surer than the pride of love (p. 97).

When Carine puts on her mask, her inner feelings of shock and fright are concretized. Her inability to differentiate between life's various personalities has made her an alienated individual. She no longer understands love, society, destiny, her Mother, Christine, or Frederic. When he approaches, Carine tears off the mask and reverts to her former self, to her pristine state of purity. In a moment of strength, Frederic orders the Dominoes out of his and Carine's lives, out of their bedroom—a sanctuary devoted to love. He seeks to return to the original state of Adam and Eve, but the world intrudes on the young lovers. "People have entered" (p. 98). The Dominoes invade the scene creating tumult by their presence. Their spasmodic rhythmic sequences and the aggressions they perpetrate on each other prepare the mood for the play's tragic finale.

IV   *Influences*

Carine, perhaps more than any other Crommelynck work, may have been inspired by the gracious yet cruel plays of Marivaux, Musset, Giraudoux, and Anouilh.

Like Marivaux, Crommelynck makes use of the *commedia dell'arte* improvisation technique in the Domino sequences. As in *Harlequin Polished by Love*, Crommelynck's Dominoes mimic, parry, or dramatize real-life situations. Marivaux's buffoon, or Harlequin, and the scintillating and brilliant nuances evoked are interwoven in Crommelynck's spectacle. The naturalness of the *commedia dell'arte* actors is apparent in the Dominoes as they pirouette, glide, fall or embrace.

The double-theme technique, characteristic in some of Marivaux's plays (as, for example, in *The Game of Love and Chance*), is also present in *Carine*. With Marivaux, the inner and outer realities rest on disguises, secret situations, love-hate relationships that evoke laughter, tears, passivity, and aggressiveness. When love is born in *The Game of Love and Chance*, it is at first hesitant, then grows despite the difficulties placed in the protagonists' path. The mixture of artifice and truth, the *sine qua non* of Marivaux's theater, is also achieved by the Dominoes in *Carine*. Each scene is rendered more acute by the mimicking of the Dominos either in keeping with or diametrically opposed to the situation being enacted. Satire and caricature of the protagonists also enliven the mood and increase the burlesque effect of the sequence. The Dominoes are like the *commedia dell'arte lazzis* who mock "eternally" passionate love scenes as well as idealize them. They emphasize the paucity of true feelings in the other protagonists by underscoring their debauched natures.

In Musset's *One Does not Joke with Love*, a situation similar to *Carine*'s is enacted. Musset's ingenue, believing in true love, sincerity, and the beauty of relationships, is deeply hurt when she discovers that her fiancé used her to win someone else's affections, and commits suicide. Crommelynck's incarnations are more expressionistic than Musset's. The Hunter, The Mother, and Christine are made of heavier fabric, deeply vice-ridden, more grotesque human beings than even the rambunctious drunks sometimes inhabiting

Musset's drama. Crommelynck's humor is Flemish. It is weighty, incisive, bleak, like the brushstrokes of Vlaminck or Van Dongen.

Giraudoux depicts the ingenue and the dangers involved in the passage from childhood to maturity in *Intermezzo* (1933) and the confrontation between the world of nature and society in *Ondine* (1939). Unlike *Intermezzo* in which an idealistic young teacher attempts to infuse a love of nature in her students, Carine is a convent-bred girl with all the fantasies and frustrations such a circumscribed education arouses. Giraudoux handles his situations with utmost tact, reserve, and subtle humor. Crommelynck's ingenue lives in a world of extremes, never able to understand her surroundings. The water nymph Ondine fell in love with a beautiful knight and died as a result of his infidelities. Carine also demands total commitment of Frederic and the others inhabiting her world. Unlike Giraudoux's theater, which is devoid of truly vicious types, Crommelynck's vision is filled with them.

Affinities with *Carine* are also present in some of Anouilh's works. In *Thieves' Ball* (1938) and *Ring Round the Moon* (1947), Anouilh introduces theatergoers to buffoon ballets that depict the inner meanderings of the psyche. The masked ball in one of Anouilh's plays adds fluidity to the entire piece, as do the Dominoes in *Carine*. Anouilh's ballets revolve around questions of class consciousness and economic differences between the participants. Crommelynck is usually indifferent to economic disparity in society and grapples more forcefully with his protagonists' psyches. Both, however, clothe the conflicts of their protagonists in pantomimic interludes that underscore the dream quality of the works.

V   *The Director: Lugné-Poë*

Crommelynck dedicated *Carine* to Lugné-Poë, who created the play's *mise-en-scène*. He admired the famous theatrical director, founder of the history-making Théâtre de l'Oeuvre (1893), because he had revolutionized theatrical design by asking painters such as Vuillard, Munch, Toulouse-Lautrec, and Bonnard to decorate his sets. Lugné-Poë was also admired by Crommelynck for his ability to discern talent. It was he who had invited Alfred Jarry to produce his

King Ubu (1896) at the Théâtre de l'Oeuvre, creating a veritable furor in theatrical circles. Lugné-Poë's open-mindedness was another of his remarkable traits. In 1893 he stated, "We will perform those works, religiously, which appear to us to be the most clever and the best conductors of ideas."[6] Lugné-Poë refused to become aligned exclusively with symbolic playwrights. "L'Oeuvre depends upon no school, and if the acceptance of mystically oriented plays has led some astray, the time to think is at hand: outside of Maeterlinck's admirable plays, symbolism has produced nothing in terms of the theater."[7] Along with André Antoine, Lugné-Poë invited foreign playwrights, such as Ibsen, Gorky, Strindberg, and Hoffmannsthal, to perform their works in ultranationalistic France.

Lugné-Poë's directing was appreciated by Crommelynck for its simple and straightforward underlying idea: that underscored the general, and not the particular.[8] The hall in which *Carine* takes place, for example, was hung with lanterns and, as in classical drama, gave the impression of being an open square or a parlor in some Italian Renaissance villa, or a general meeting room. A staircase with a wrought-iron banister hung with foliage stood in the background. The balcony and a white-walled gallery were also visible, giving the stage added dimension, depth and a sense of the collective. A table placed centerstage and brocaded chairs on either side lent an aristocratic flavor to the set, reminiscent of a Watteau canvas.

Although some of the themes dramatized in *Carine* may be said to by pedestrian, the depth of the characterizations and the variety between existential situations and the Domino sequences make Crommelynck's work an artistic theatrical event.

CHAPTER 7

Hot and Cold:
Expressionism and the Mythmaking
Principle (1934)

*H*OT and Cold is a three-act comedy farce. Its humor is lowbrow, hard, and cruel; its pace, vigorous; its repartees, acerbic. *Hot and Cold* is also a paradigm of expressionistic theater. It is a play in which the mythmaking principle is viewed as a working and viable phenomenon.

Hot and Cold was well received when it opened on November 20, 1934, at the Comédie des Champs-Elysées, despite some dissenting voices. Paul Achard of *Ami du Peuple* considered it "incontestably a great play, one of Crommelynck's best . . . curious, endearing, original"; Gérard Bauer of *Les Nouvelles Littéraires* found "the colorful tone of the dialogue" original and reminiscent of "joyful Flemish realism"; Pierre Brisson of *Le Figaro* looked upon it as a "strange amalgam of artifice and sincerity"; Jacques Copeau believed it to be cumbersome with a "surplus of themes"; Pierre Lièvre of *Jour* wrote that it was a "confused blend of subtleties and crudities"; Emile Mass in *Petit Bleu* suggested that Crommelynck's characters were like "marionnettes who never stopped chatting away."[1] When revived in 1956, *Hot and Cold* gave rise to even more strongly divided reviews: Jean Guignebert of *Libération* found it "hard, cruel, vigorous, and devoid of all complacencies"; Robert Kemp of *Le Monde* declared that it was passé, "fettered comedy where even exuberance was calculated and humor made heavy"; Max Favalelli of *Paris Presse* was convinced that *Hot and Cold* was of eternal value: "It will still be alive while others, whom we laud to the heavens today, will long have become dried mummies."[2]

119

I *The Plot*

Hot and Cold tells the story of M. Dom's wife, Léona, who finds her husband dull and prosaic. She has therefore taken a series of lovers: Thierry, Bellemasse, Odilon. Each time she tires of one, which happens frequently, she elicits the aid of her clever servant Alix to free her from the unwanted suitor. Odilon, the latest in line, is so passionately in love with Léona that he threatens to poison M. Dom. He does not need to carry out his intention. As fate would have it M. Dom is brought home one afternoon in a semicomatose condition. Shortly before his demise a young attractive girl, Félie, enters M. Dom's home in great distress. Unbeknown to Léona, she had been M. Dom's mistress for ten years. Her pride hurt, Léona grows jealous of Félie's past happiness and is angered by her husband's hypocritical attitude toward her. Alix, aware of Léona's suffering, tries to distract her and spreads the rumor that just before he died, M. Dom said: "I have an idea." This statement spreads throughout the town like wildfire. It is magnified to such an extent that M. Dom is transformed into a hero. Léona, meanwhile, tries to get rid of Félie. She forces Odilon to seduce her, and the ruse works. Félie is no longer interested in M. Dom's memory nor in his "Spiritual legacy," which has turned into a credo. The new "belief" gives Léona's life purpose and teaches her the meaning of love. She can now admire M. Dom and proudly say that she has come out the victor: "He is mine, completely mine." Her relationship with her husband was cold during his lifetime but is now hot after his death. An altar will be set up in her home that will be a sanctuary where homage may be paid to the founder of the Domist cult.

II *Crommelynck's Brand of Expressionism*

Expressionist theater, defined traditionally as a subjective representation of a personal vision of humanity, enabled Crommelynck to create in *Hot and Cold* a ribald satire deriding and caricaturizing people in need of a cult and cult objects. The female protagonist is the drama's pivotal force: all situations, climaxes, and the dénouement radiate and coalesce as a result of her needs, deficiencies, and qualities.

The play is written in the expressionist tradition of Strindberg, Wedekind, Lenormand, and Kokoshka—but with a comic twist. It therefore elicits a pathological laughter from audiences. Events and personalities as viewed through the eyes of Léona are distorted, offensive, and bewildering. The repressive and bigoted forces at work in society are powerfully and sardonically denigrated. Although Crommelynck's language is poetic, even lyrical at times— particularly during the love-duet interludes—its beauty is hard, cold, and puppetlike, underscoring the inability of man to communicate with his fellow beings on even the most superficial of levels. An abraded world is embodied for the viewer.

Unlike Realism and Naturalism, Expressionism explores personality traits and social inadequacies on an impersonal level. Ibsen, Zola, and Brieux fought specific social evils, whereas Crommelynck and Strindberg were enraged by general wrongs. In *A Dream Play*, for example, Strindberg depicts society through the dream of Indra's daughter, who enters the earthly sphere to better comprehend the ways of man. In Wedekind's *Spring Awakening*, the community is rejected through the family cell and its failure to properly educate the young protagonist. To reinforce his anger, Wedekind has his actors proclaim their lines in an unrealistic, impersonal manner, exaggerating every word, phrase, and clause, thus reflecting through rhythmic and tonic structures the hardness and frigidity of the characters. Oskar Kokoshka's ire against the sexes, as revealed in *Murderer, Hope of Women*, is expelled in bursts of hysteria by his characters; though the dialogue is frequently incomprehensible, the explosive delivery is a direct outgrowth of the personalities' chaotic inner architecture.

Hot and Cold not only depicts the faulty values in the marriage structure, but also the vacuous nature of society in general: its need for illusion, for the lie, for a credo or banner that will take people out of themselves—a placebo. Léona and the world from which she emerges are viewed by Crommelynck as empty, destructive entities. Those who function in this framework do so with a kind of macabre hilarity—black humor that, as defined by André Breton, banishes all sentimentality and tenderness, and is therefore difficult to understand and even more difficult to appreciate.[3]

Crommelynck has combined Expressionism and comedy to point up society's foibles as well as to discredit his protagonist and her entourage. In *Hot and Cold*, the "ugly" comes to the fore; that element which, according to Aristotle, makes for the "ridiculous."[4] To the *ugly* and the *ridiculous* may be added a third element, the *absurd*. Crommelynck's situations are absurd, as are those dramatized by Ionesco in his "tragic farces." Indeed, Ionesco has expressed himself on the subject of comedy as being quite close to tragedy:

In that comedy is the intuition of the absurd, it seem to me far more despairing than tragedy. Comedy offers no way out. I say: "despairing," but in reality it goes far beyond—or above—despair or hope.[5]

In *The Bald Soprano*, Ionesco mocks some of society's activities, its "normal" comportment, and the banalities uttered throughout people's lives. The laughter aroused is derisive, contradictory, violent, yet quite natural. In *Hot and Cold*, the same kind of grinding rictus is elicited from the audience because the world Crommelynck depicts bathes in "strangeness," and in a series of "clichés" that may be viewed as quite depressing.

Although not "worse than the average," Crommelynck's protagonists become the target for satire. Léona is a fire principle and represents blind amorality. Therefore, the resulting humor cannot be linked to the merriment derived from Plautus's comedies, *The Haunted House* and *The Rope*, in which lively love affairs and confusion abound; nor may it be compared to Terence's sprightly works, *Eunuchus* and *Phormio*, in which the characters in all of their subtle vagaries arouse bouts of laughter in the viewer. A certain healthiness and spirited verve are evinced in these ancient comedies: a judicious outcome reinforces the ludicrous and impossible pattern of events.[6]

Crommelynck's expressionist comedy is nihilistic and despairing. Léona never experiences any kind of conflict in terms of her behavior. She never struggles to suppress certain tendencies within her or to resolve what gnaws at her. Her inhibitions are perpetually bubbling on the surface. No reason or critical judgment and no power of evaluation or perception ever emerge. The world of this type of superficial and sordid individual thrives on excitement generated by every new incident. It pursues its peripheral course and lives for and by web-spinning or mythmaking.

Thus, life as experienced by Léona is bare, devoid of meaning, and, although comic, is in effect a humiliating tragedy. Unlike the existentialist dramatist Camus, whose characters attempt to face themselves, Léona skirts surfaces and finds extravagant ways of relieving the routine axis of her life. Her lovers, she hopes, will bring her some kind of *élan vital,* some semblance of merriment and joy. The rate at which she changes them, however, attests to her own failure; such activity does not give birth to a long-term solution. Her lies, deceits, and slanders usher in what expressionist dramatists view as a paradigm of the ugliness of man's soul, the paucity of his vision, and the inferior nature of his being. Although one might argue that the protagonists in Camus' *The Misunderstanding* and *Caligula* or in Sartre's *No Exit* and *The Devil and the Good Lord* are similarly gruesome, they demonstrate nevertheless courage and willingness to muster their energies in an attempt to confront their inner beings—their smudged souls—thus creating a more lucid but not necessarily happier vision of life. Even in Lenormand's plays *Time is a Dream* and *The Simoon,* in which man's pathetic and nihilistic nature is examined and exteriorized, and is found to be bereft of beauty, one is made privy to a redemptive quality, a metaphysical grandeur resulting from the experience and the pain implicit in it. In *Man and His Ghosts* and *The Eater of Dreams,* Lenormand depicts a world in which neuroses, incest, murder, and sexual anomalies of all types are the corpus of the drama, but so is man's desire to transcend his negative destiny.

In *Hot and Cold* no positive ideas emerge; the characters are carried along by their vices. The slow erosion of a personality is viewed as a humorous state of affairs. Thus, grotesque and farcelike beings people Crommelynck's stage, forever circumventing truth and accepting illusion. Their mythmaking power and the resultant cult becomes a palliative. *Hot and Cold,* or the dramatization of life built on egotism, deceit, and the acceptance of subterfuges by an individual and a community, results in a side-splitting joke. Léona

becomes a kind of master of ceremonies, a *psychopomp*, a leader of
the game called life—in which man puts something over on himself.

III   *The Psychopomp and the Unicellular Hetaera*

Léona, the psychopomp, or *meneur de jeu*, is a hetaera woman.
The hetaera is a courtesan type: beautiful, entertaining, charming,
and understandably bored with a husband whom she considers prosaic and physically revolting. The hetaera has existed since the
world began. In Greece she was associated with Aphrodite worship
and was introduced into society by ordinance of Solon. Her function
was to see to the pleasures of unmarried men, thereby preventing
any threat to the structure of marriage. Many hetaera women were
well-known for their refined and exquisite ways and men of renown
were attracted to them. Aspasia of Miletus drew to her the most
extraordinary of men, including Socrates and Pericles, the latter
abandoning his legal wife to marry her. There were other hetaerae:
Semiramis, Cleopatra, Diane de Poitiers, Jeanne d'Aragon. The
hetaera is a collective figure: the source of pleasure, energy, life.
She has come to encompass an ideal because it is by her charms that
man indulges in the sexual and creative act, that he feels forever
young and is eternally reborn. She has positive attributes in that she
may act as man's companion on an intellectual, spiritual, and sexual
level—and become a *femme inspiratrice*. On the other hand, the
hetaera may be a destructive force when playing the role of seduc-
tress, attracting the man away from his chosen destiny and his
wife—as does the *femme fatale*.

Léona is a *femme fatale*. Women such as she are all things to all
men. For Thierry she took on the stature of a goddess; for
Bellemasse, she was a divine object; for Odilon, a corporeal sen-
sualist. She ordered them about as she saw fit and they yielded to
her will; spellbound, they became votaries of this powerful force.

Onomastically Léona—which comes from the Latin *leo,leonis*,
"lion"—resembles the animal. She has lionlike force; a kind of solar
energy and courage that enable her to destroy what she thinks to be
inimical to her needs. The lion (which figures on the French, German, and English coat of arms) not only represents power, but an
irascible appetite, instinctual force, avidity, and vigor as well. In

many myths and fairy tales the lion has been equated with the dragon who protects great treasures (the "Lion Knight" in the Arthurian cycle, for example) and in this instance uses all means, whether brutal or not, to gain his ends. Implicit in Léona are these cruel, tension-filled, and ruinous features. She is an aggressive, energizing, excitable element, and her flamboyant or flamelike ways are a replica of her inner being. Throughout the play she acts in a chaotic, demonstrative, and episodic manner. Her disorderly nature causes the play's jagged structure. The scenes frequently give the impression of improvisation; the characters forever barge in and out in a quite acausal nature; the dialogue is interrupted by the sudden appearance and disappearance of characters; and bursts of anger from Léona's rejected suitors also impose themselves spasmodically on the stage happenings. The derision provoked by Léona's emotional upheavals or Alix's eruptions into the picture trigger off protests from other characters, not only adding to the suspense factor, but also creating a series of rhythmic and imagistic reverberations. Although only Léona's voice dominates the situations enacted, a plurality of voices is heard as cacophonous background music, all of which is integrated into the Crommelynckian construct.

We are first introduced to Léona through Ida, Thierry's jilted wife. She erupts onto the stage ready to tear Léona apart with her bare hands: "It won't be the first time," she screams, that 'the beautiful Léona' will be beaten. She will pay for having taken him and leaving him."

Alix is also rambunctious. As a kind of alter ego for Léona, she too is a catalyst. Her namesake, Alix de Champagne, Queen of France and wife of Louis VII (1160), mother of the illustrious Philip Augustus, is transformed by Crommelynck into a servant, thus discrediting what had been highly valued: queenship. It is Alix's obligation to play hide-and-seek with Bellemasse, another of Léona's rejected lovers. As planned by the two ladies but still unbeknown to the audience, Léona finds Alix and Bellemassse ensconced in an armchair, kissing madly. Léona wears a mask of anger and hurt, thus deceiving her suitor and audiences who believe her pain to be real. The entire amorous escapade is handled with *brio* and permits Léona on grounds of *flagrante delicto* to rid herself of Bellemasse.

As a final flourish, she allows her fiery temperament to explode, thus compelling him to depart. Léona now flits about the stage in a joyful interlude as she awaits her next lover, Odilon. Alix remarks, thus including the audience in their complicity: "It is so pleasurable to change men. One effaces the other."

To Odilon, Léona makes known her needs and the course her love will take: "You will work for me, for both of us?" (p. 255). And the cumbersome, awkward bumpkin believes her passion to be real and lasting. As in *The Marriage of Figaro*, the entire scene with Odilon rests on a series of skirmishes and *contretemps*—the fool and the clever hetaera—the one acting in all sincerity, though a bit dull-witted in his ways, the other basking in her delightful machinations, in her quest and conquest. The motility of the sequences featuring Odilon and Léona depends upon the points of controversy at stake and their resolution.

As Odilon's passion grows, so does his jealousy of M. Dom. Wearying of Odilon's ardor, Léona assures him there are no grounds for jealousy. Then she turns around and humiliates him by asking him to go on an errand for her; to further irritate him, she adds insidiously: "And what will I do to forget you while you're away? I'll deceive you" (p. 258). Odilon reacts as she expected; he threatens to kill her. But his fury merely heightens her sexual joy, which now grows to unparalleled heights.

M. Dom's death does not subdue Odilon's temper. He is so outraged by Léona's obsession with her late husband's memory that he is ready to strike her. To relieve the tension and inject humor into the sequence, Alix pokes her head through a window and screeches: "Yes, strike, strike, strike her!" (p. 294). The comic interruption, of course, has the opposite effect. Odilon stops short and falls into the armchair in shock and disbelief, humiliated at the thought that another has witnessed his emotional display.

M. Dom's death arouses Léona's anger. Her wounded pride, her gullibility at her husband's deceit, and her jealousy over the happiness he had experienced with Félie alter her opinion of him. Indeed, she is caught up in Félie's lyricism, in her passionate love and devotion to his memory, and responds dramatically to the image created by the rival. M. Dom begins to attain epic grandeur in

Léona's imagination. And as her admiration increases, the once flighty, superficial, and amoral hetaera is transformed into a statuesque, elegant kind of vestal virgin. Her house becomes a Domist sanctuary, and in the last scene, fills with guests come to pay homage to the great M. Dom. Thierry, once her lover but now the apostle of a new religion, suggests that "The Altar to the Idea" be built in the home. "These three steps seem to have been placed here for this express purpose." The room will be elevated, isolated, and thus a "special solemnity" will be conferred on it. The burgomaster speaks of the rituals involved in Domist worship and the heights of spirituality these may attain. Thirty delegations are to arrive and declare themselves Domists. As the crowd enters, Léona, caught up in the Domist myth, confesses to Alix that she has finally found love; her soul now experiences its true calling. In a burst of lyrical frenzy, she glorifies M. Dom's new image and the lasting love to which it has led.

Crommelynck's satire of organized religion and of the hetaera type is comparable in its biting humor to Boccaccio's *Decameron*, a collection of narratives in which the amoral, crude, and vicious side of mankind is played up; it is also comparable to some of Chaucer's *Canterbury Tales*, where the lascivious maidens, bent upon sensual rather than spiritual pleasures, materialize their desires. Crommelynck's brand of Expressionism draws upon the inner and outer ugliness of individuals, their bestiality and cruelty, their distorted views of life. These are then incised into his drama in the manner of Nolde or Kokoshka—a world bereft of tenderness and sensitivity.

IV *The Mythmaking Factor*

The myth, considered as a primordial experience not necessarily personal but rather transcendental, is delineated in *Hot and Cold* in sequential situations that are then organized into macro- and microstructures. The events making up the myth are fleshed out during the course of the drama. Each event shuttles between the aforementioned polarities, thus building up momentum as it is enacted onstage, and finally becoming interlocked in its construct. The result: the transformation of what was an amorphous and passive "idea" into a vital and positive force capable of bringing about the well-being of the protagonist and the community from which she emerges.

When Genet created his myth in *The Screens,* it took on the dimension of a religious ritual; it enabled the votaries within its framework to take on stature, to step away from their mortal sphere and penetrate the immortal realm, the individual to the transcendental. Genet's view is, however, ambivalent. Although he takes seriously man's mystical quests and the rituals inherent in these, he nevertheless is able to objectivize and satirize man's inability to come to grips with the notion of death and to face the fact that he needs illusion to pursue his life. Crommelynck's mythmaking process is strictly a ruse, a hoax, a joke humanity plays upon itself in order to be able to walk about the earth blind and deaf to its realities. It is a satiric-comic view of life. Genet is spiritually oriented; Crommelynck is earth-centered. His life is firmly rooted on and in matter and not in some nebulous spatial, celestial, or infernal sphere.

M. Dom is, unwittingly, the catalyst for the mythmaking process. Onomastically Dom comes from the Latin *dominus,* "master." It was a title given in the Middle Ages, Renaissance, and Classical era to certain men of religion; it was also an honorary title attributed to nobles in Portugal. In fact, when Molière wrote his *Dom Juan,* he spelled it *Dom* and not, as later interpreters insisted, *Don.* In addition, *D.O.M.* is an abbreviation for the Latin *Deo optimo, maximo,* "To God the best, the greatest," a formula used to dedicate religious edifices.

By using the name Dom, which lends historicity, continuity, and religious overtones to the play, Crommelynck was carefully setting the stage. He prepared the terrain for the mythmaking process. The fact that M. Dom never appears onstage, that he dies in some mysterious manner, and that the details surrounding his life are never subsumed, inject an aura around his being. He takes on the attributes and dimensions of a remote divinity, a kind of powerful father figure who will dominate all the events in the play.

A countermovement also comes into being. Léona, who had considered her husband pedantic and had been a seducer of men, is now transformed—through religion—into a dignified priestess of sorts, a female votary to the new Domist cult. Whereas Félie, who had loved M. Dom for ten years in secret and knew felicity during his lifetime (as her name indicates), takes on another aspect after his death. Onomastically Félie is feline, catlike. She insinuates her way into Léona's house, into its activities. Félie is also a felon; she betrays her dead lover. Seduced by Odilon, thanks to Léona's machinations, Félie becomes an apostate. She rejects Domism and its cult for the dead in favor of the alive, attractive, virile Odilon.

The mythmaking mechanism is expertly interwoven into the fabric of the play. The nuances of Léona's anger, jealousy, and feelings of rejection are countered by M. Dom's growing reputation through the rumors that declare him an unrecognized genius, the creator of an idea the townspeople interpret as a boon to humanity. As is the case of most cult objects or patriarchal images, M. Dom becomes a kind of placebo—a hierophany—capable of solving all of life's problems. The collective psychosis so brilliantly evoked by Jules Romains in *Dr. Knock* (where the doctor through the power of suggestion controls the personalities of a group of mountain people) and in *Crommedeyre-le-vieil* (where some kidnapped girls are assimilated into the substance of some remote village) is dramatized step by step by Crommelynck—leading to collective intoxication.

The energy generated by M. Dom's *idea* (which is never elucidated upon), concocted by Alix in order to dispel Léona's wounded ego, takes on the power of an avalanche. M. Dom's genius arouses the admiration of the burgomaster, the teacher, and the political leaders of the community. His doctrine—ultravague—influences neighboring towns until a mob psychology comes into being. Like a plague, news travels quickly; instant communication is experienced as the gullible adopt the new religion; the masses and the irrational element predominate as the promise of a *fontaine de jouvence* is offered to everyone who converts to Domism.

"M. Dom's ideas have conquered the entire province," (p. 332), Léona states, herself overwhelmed by the greatness of her late husband. A veritable epiphany occurs, a miracle that gives authenticity and stature to the newly created religion. On the third day after M. Dom's death rumors have it that he appeared in various towns and districts. "M. Dom passed through Villou and Beauvisu and

Pranet—he is at this moment at Terres-Meubles." To reinforce the
mythico-religious flavor of the miraculous event, Alix intones: "The
morning of the third day." Thus, Crommelynck satirizes Christ's
resurrection on the third day while also derogating organized religion and the power it holds over humanity (p. 309–10).

As events near their climactic finale, each county seat articulates
its own interpretation of Domist doctrine, setting up dialectical situations: "The doctrine ennunciated by the Jury committee is diametrically opposed to ours, without its being any the less Domist" (p.
339). The "spiritual legacy" is of such value to the various people
involved and to the communities they represent, they are filled with
emotion as they talk of the new cult. Léona, the guiding spiritual
force now, the mystical queen of Domism, accepts her new role as
religious leader of the community. Statuesque in her black gown,
her visage now wears the countenance of saintliness and is marked
by deep gravity.

Theatrically speaking, Crommelynck maintains the stage conventions as had Giraudoux, Vildrac, Romains, and Anouilh. Plot therefore is important: suspense, climax, and dénouement. Language is
not devalued as in the works of the Surrealists and Absurdists,
although it is used as a weapon to bombard, shock, and disorient;
nor is any attempt made to create a new stage language or hieroglyphics as advocated by Antonin Artaud. Crommelynck's theater is
not antiliterary as is Ionesco's. It has not rejected empathy as has
Genet; nor anthropomorphism as has Adamov; nor does it indulge in
alienation, a technique used with such felicity by Brecht. Unlike the
works of Genet, Beckett, and Ionesco, *Hot and Cold* is devoid of
metaphysical anguish; it does not proceed via symbols, nor is it
focused on solving problems. Life and people as viewed by Crommelynck are devoid of a code of ethics, and if they constitute one, it
is at best only temporary and rarely adhered to. Ideals are de-
valuated. The human condition is looked upon as irrational, motivations as amoral.

Crommelynck's theater is one of violence insofar as man's needs
and personality are concerned. It is violent in its situations, semiotics, gestures, and stage movement. Crommelynck's speech, his

situations, and his characters are objects: wooden, hard, unbending. However, they are lyrical at times, for instance, when experiencing love crises. Odilon reveals his passion to Léona: "I knew that our bodies would join each other immediately, even despite ourselves." Félie expresses her love: "Adorable day: the flowers brighten as at dusk, the shadow takes on a spangled hue under the trees, and I saw groups of flying ants displaying their golden halo in the valley!" Seconds later their words become choppy, frigid, and brittle, like hammer strokes, when Léona discovers her husband's treachery: "Am I not strong, supple, alert, determined . . . the furor of my glance . . . Not one blink! And here I am: hatred nourishes me!" (pp. 256, 328, 290). Harsh effects are now dealt out visually and acoustically as rhythms accelerate and groups of staccatolike enumerations follow, each mounting in intensity. Language explodes at times and becomes a quasiautonomous factor in the stage happenings.

I want her punished: And you heard me say it, the burgomaster's interdict; Félie will not enter the cemetery; never, I swear to you! Close the window! And go on, run! Félie will leave! Ha! . . . Just as love drew and quartered me, so will hatred! Tell Odilon that they will discover us grafted, soldered, healed to all love wounds! . . . My furor will deliver me or I'll smother! (315).

Crommelynck uses linguistic devices to discredit Léona and her entourage: antitheses and repetitions ("hatred, hatred, hatred"), slang phrases ("the trollop," in French *la garce*), neologisms (Domism), clichés ("I have plunged into love as a swimmer in water" (p. 245), and puns ("Ephé-mère") (p. 300). He uses onomatopoeias semiotically to inject character traits into the visual image: "More slippery than an eel!" (p. 286). "A real slimy eel!" (p. 289). A signified and signifier blend into one when Léona's hatred is described in terms of ice: "Nothing but pure, naked hatred, salubrious as the air of glaciers" will help her face her ordeal (p. 292). Language gave birth to M. Dom's *idea*, and its "spiritual legacy" to mankind is the generating principle around this absurd yet paradoxically plausible play.

Although *Hot and Cold* is built on the causality principle, that is, on an initial situation and its resolution—including the evolution of its characters and progression in terms of the events delineated—it is far more than a conventional comedy. The structural basis for the mythmaking process is expressionistic, and thus audiences are made privy to a world viewed from the standpoint of a single protagonist; the resulting constructs are, however, exceedingly tightly knit, each scene solidly built into the next, like geological folds. Moreover, events and signs reveal a rhythmic pattern and code that veer from the personal to the collective, thus enabling the dramatist to point up the ribaldry and humor implicit in certain scenes. To have written a comedy with such *brio* revolving around the theme of disenchantment and the notion of death, to have caricaturized the characters by aggrandizing their ugliness and distorted views, to have depotentiated religion and the mythmaking process and evoked laughter throughout the stage happenings is to corroborate Nell's statement in Beckett's *Endgame*: "Nothing is funnier than unhappiness . . . Yes, yes, it's the most comical thing in the world."

CHAPTER 8

A Woman Whose Heart Is too Small: *The Would-Be Dominant (1934)*

A LTHOUGH theatrically speaking, *A Woman Whose Heart Is too Small* is not innovative, the power of the play's satire, the outlandish nature of its central character, and the spirited dynamism of its theme make it arresting comedy. This time Crommelynck singles out the ultramoralistic woman, the overly virtuous female whose ways are so ordered as to resemble an automaton and whose attitude is so authoritarian as to spread solemnity. She evokes laughter because her actions and points of view are "designed not to condemn evil, but to ridicule a lack of self-knowledge."[1] For Crommelynck, the protagonist represents the new twentieth-century woman, the petty bourgeoise, the kind of female he must have despised: superficial, intransigent, and devoid of feeling.

When first produced at the Théâtre de l'Oeuvre on January 15, 1934, under the direction of Pauline Pax, the reviews were mixed. Etienne Ray of *Comoedia*[2] considered the play prolix and too overly complex to be absorbing and humorous. Thomas-Nitchevo of *Matin Belge*[3] found it entrancing, its ribaldry tittilating, and its characterizations acerbic and worthy of a Molière. When the play was revived in 1942 in occupied Paris, it fell on deaf ears. The theme of the woman who places hollow morality above human understanding seemed dated. Considering the irony of the situations and the comedy of manners set side by side with the political and economic suffering of France during the German occupation and under the Pétain régime, *A Woman Whose Heart Is too Small* was out of place. Plays dramatizing conflicts concerning commitment or metaphysical

133

anguish brought about by solitude and death were more appropriate. Sartre's *The Flies* (1943), which deals with the absurdity of
existence and the authentic action of individuals, answered that
need; so did Anouilh's *Antigone* (1943), whose heroine is willing to
suffer death for her ideals; and Camus' *Caligula* (1944), which de-
lineates the tragic fate of a man who seeks to exploit his power even
if it means the systematic destruction of all values, including love
and friendship. *A Woman Whose Heart Is too Small* seemed trivial
by comparison. Yet, there is something to be said for Crommelynck's masterful theatrical hand. The banal acquires new dimension. The characters, all subservient to the protagonist, are pushed
to the extreme of credibility and thus take on the drollery of
Rabelais' Gargantua and Panurge. Exaggeration, a mainstay of
Rabelaisian humor, is also a factor in the portrayal of Crommelynck's
eccentric creatures who foment intrigue and lighthearted banter in a
truculent and imagistic dialogue.

I *The Plot*

A Woman Whose Heart Is too Small opens in a large family room
on an Italian-style country estate. Olivier, a widower, his charming
daughter Patricia, her friend Isabelle, and two servants, Minna and
Xantus, live in an unconstrained and happy atmosphere. Then Balbine, Olivier's new wife, arrives. Rather than add zest and humor to
a cheerful household, she accomplishes the opposite. A combination
of prude and prig, and intransigent with regard to household mat-
ters, Balbine sets off a series of unpleasant chain reactions. She
insists that the house be spotless at all times, that the cushions be
puffed up, that the servants work relentlessly. She is a woman who
lives on theory alone—and a negative theory at that. She rejects sex
and does not understand the heart. She never allows feelings of love
to guide her. Like Tartuffe's credo, hers is based on false virtue and
false religious intent. Her catechism is negative. She feels it is un-
wise, for example, to allow Patricia to stray from the house. Because
this healthy young girl is compelled to remain a virtual prisoner, her
fantasy life begins to work overtime. She invents a story about an
Italian lover who comes to visit her nightly in her room. When
Balbine hears of this and believes it—she considers it an erotic,

perverse, and degrading affair. To right a wrong, she forces Patricia to marry the timid agronomist Gabriel, a kind of poet-dreamer, a charming Pierrot figure. Unbeknown to Balbine, Gabriel has been in love with Patricia but was too timid to ask for her hand in marriage. As for the servants, they are reprimanded. Minna's dress is too revealing, Xantus's affections are too overt. They are forced into constraint: the naturalness and ease of their former relationship is made to appear dirty, their ways sullied. And Olivier, not experiencing the marital bliss he had anticipated, becomes hypochondriacal and despondent. Balbine demands that they have separate rooms and that he take his temperature every hour. The situation finally becomes untenable. Like Petruccio in *The Taming of the Shrew*, Olivier takes the situation in hand. He resorts to deception and remains out all night, returning the following morning and playing drunk. She accuses him of carousing with other men and of violating Minna. Balbine is beside herself with dismay. Her heart is too small to understand the larger aspects of life. All ends well, however, as Olivier takes over and his household resumes its normal and cheerful course.

II *Characterizations*

In an interview, Crommelynck declared that staging and decor were merely functions of a play; cf primary importance was "the dramatic substance, that is, everything that acts, speaks"—the characters.[4] Like Molière, Crommelynck attempted to peer into the depths of certain types of people, to learn about those mysterious realms where souls are haunted by passion, where motivations and obsessions take root. Crommelynck's and Molière's method was to bring these various eccentricities or phobias to light by blowing them out of proportion in the incidents dramatized, thus drawing attention to the importance of the conflict at that particular moment. As are Molière's, Crommelynck's characters are true to life; they are based on observation. The seventeenth-century master of comedy described it in the following words:

When you paint heroes, you can do as you wish; they are portraits created for pleasure and one does not search for resemblance: but when you paint men, you must paint them according to nature.[5]

Balbine is reminiscent of Molière's *Intellectual Women*. They are as absurd and comic in their "excessive purism in grammar and diction and the tendency to be idiotic in precision" as Balbine is in her meticulous cleanliness, religious orthodoxy, and rejection of sex. Because she lives by principle alone, her authoritarian and overly moralistic ways encourage vice rather than virtue, hate rather than love, and pain rather than pleasure. No matter what she undertakes, whether it be in connection with human relationships, her exaggerated notions and dogmatic ways are grotesque; thus they are food for laughter. The statement George Meredith made about Molière's art could be applied to Crommelynck's.

He seized his characters firmly for the central purpose of the play, stamped them in the idea, and, by slightly raising and softening the object of study (as in the case of the ex-Huguenot, Duke de Montausier, for the study of the Misanthrope, and, according to Saint-Simon, the Abbé Roquette for Tartuffe), generalized upon it so as to make it permanently human.[6]

Balbine's household must be immaculate. Dirt must vanish; the wash must be snow-white. The servants must work continuously. This combination of cerebral and overly meticulous woman makes of her a strictly Cartesian type: where order and reason reign supreme, all else falls into place. Emotion never intrudes in Balbine's way of life. If it did, then so would the chance factor and with it, perhaps, discord. Therefore, all had to be well regulated to avoid any intervention of *hazard*; had to be carried out with method.

Balbine's attitude is in keeping with the Bergsonian definition of comedy. Her life has become routine, her existence devoid of vitality. A pervasive sameness and predictability accompany all of her activities. For Bergson, the intent of comedy is to break the routine, to eclipse the rules of logic and to substitute the unexpected, the shocking—emotional responses. With the intrusion of unusual situations or the element of surprise, life can no longer be reduced to a formula. Such rejection of ossified and stratified concepts allows the "game factor" to intervene, thus introducing a lightness of touch, a spirit of banter and levity.[7] Balbine's somber world of microcleanliness and microsanctity would then vanish and she might, for the first time, be able to live *authentically*. It is the dramatist's function to point up the ridiculous nature of extreme behavior; hence, Crommelynck mocks her pompous attitudes and derides her pedantic ways, underscoring at the same time her inability to adapt to life.

Even the choice of her name is humorous and touches upon her salient characteristic. Balbine may be associated with the French verb *balbutier*, "to stammer" or "stutter." Such a definition characterizes her personality. She is weak-egoed and unconsciously chooses to live in an overly structured, ultrarigid world. She hides behind set credos and takes refuge behind narrow moralitic concepts. She is dominated by a ruling passion and is unable to face situations naturally because she lacks understanding of life and thus direction in her ways. Her lack of faith in mankind as well as in herself compels her to stumble along throughout a variety of situations. A paradigm of human weakness, she is a woman caught in the contradictions set forth by an obsolete credo and an unproductive life. The comedy factor arises from the disarray created when reason becomes devoid of common sense.

At the outset of the drama, Olivier describes Balbine to his brother, Constant. He tells him she fills a need in his life as his world has grown empty because his daughter is growing up and will soon "abandon the house." Then he would be alone, compelled to live on past memories and hopes.

Objects have become discolored, and stranger still, my eyes no longer see the depth and volume of the walls around me; it was as if matter clung to its mass because of some pre-arranged agreement (p. 183).

Constant calls Olivier a sentimental mystic. When Olivier tells him of his newfound happiness because of his marriage to Balbine, audiences are prepared for the most extraordinary of creatures to walk onstage.

> Olivier: She is sleeping in my house. She will
> care for it. Yes, Balbine whom I love
> is here. She is wise, joyous, chaste,
> measured in her ways. She is a well-

> protected flame who reassures me. She will
> guide us all in order and devotion.
> Constant: . . . in certitude, frankness, discretion.
> Olivier: Yes!
> Constant: . . . obliging, economical, persevering.
> Olivier: Yes and yes! (pp. 183–4).

Just as Molière paved the way for Tartuffe's emergence on the stage, so the groundwork is laid for Balbine's grand entrance. To further point up the dichotomy between fact and fantasy—or according to Schopenhauer's definition of the comic situation, between the "expected" and "the real object"[8]—Patricia and Isabelle come forth. Their arms are filled with roses and their laughter resounds throughout the house. Just at this moment Balbine enters—and instead of the feminine, maternal, and delicate creature we expect, we are introduced to a cold, rigid, and brusque woman. She is wearing her husband's old clothes: baggy pants, boots far too large, and an old gardener's hat. She emerges as a distortion, a caricature, of the picture of perfection Olivier had delineated—proving once again that love is blind.

Intransigent and cerebral, Balbine is the harbinger of chaos, not cosmos. Although her harsh and rational ways are exaggerated, they are true to life, as is Molière's misanthropic Alceste, whose attitude also verges on the pathetic, and whose purity opposes the ways of society—yet elicits laughter. In "An Essay on Comedy," George Meredith wrote:

And to love Comedy you must know the real world, and to know men and women well enough not to expect too much of them, though you may still hope for the good.[9]

Balbine has some virtues, and Olivier is aware of them. She is frank, discreet, and economical. She could be the model wife if she allowed herself the liberty of being herself. Instead, she permits her brain—her rational principle—to dominate. She does all those things she thinks are right and carries to the extreme her moralistic credo, therefore ushering in disaster. Balbine is the perfect example of the anti-Rousseau individual, the one born pure whom civilization ruined. Her regime is absolutism; tyranny imposed upon herself and her entourage. Her puritanical upbringing results in the creation of hostility instead of affection. George Meredith put it as follows:

Hereditary Puritanism regarding the stage is met, to this day, in many families quite undistinguished by arrogant piety. It has subsided altogether as a power in the profession of morality; but it is an error to suppose it extinct, and unjust also to forget that it had once good reason to hate, to shun, to rebuke our public shows.[10]

Balbine's misplaced morality destroys the unconstrained atmosphere that reigned. It brings tension and anger. Worse, it defeats its own purpose by compelling Patricia to lie, Olivier to enact the role of a drunken rake, and the servants to become thieves. Balbine is as incapable of understanding Patricia's need for affection and her emerging womanhood as she is of her husband's need for warmth and love. The comic effects reside in the lengths to which she carries her morality and the ridiculous nature of the results. She fits into Aristotle's scheme for comedy:

. . . an imitation of men worse than the average; worse, however, not as regards one particular kind, the Ridiculous, which is a species of Ugly. The ridiculous may be defined as a mistake or deformity not productive of pain or harm to others; the mask, for instance, that excites laughter, is something ugly and distorted without causing pain.[11]

Balbine is not a tragic figure as, according to Rousseau, is Alceste; but she is ludicrous because she is the cause for elicit sexuality, deception, and fraud, those particular characteristics she attempts to suppress. She is so grotesque in her demeanor (both physically and morally) that she looks like a clown, a monument to foolishness. She is made to look ridiculous in other scenes; for example, when she is caught sleepwalking by the servants. She comes onstage in her nightshirt with her hair disheveled, and because she has tended to the coal stove in the cellar, she is covered with soot. Balbine

sweeps the floor and dusts about, doing all the chores of her servants. Humorous, too, is her pantomimic routine when she sleep-
walks. The variety and ingenuity of gestures are reminiscent of the
medieval jugglers' routine as they entertained the lords and ladies.[12] Balbine goes to great lengths to wipe each of the window-
panes: she breathes on the glass, rubs it, then walks away to verify
its transparency. When she begins to sweep she takes great care not
to make dust each time she moves a piece of furniture. Her facial
expressions suit the humor of her activities. Intent upon completing
her tasks, she stares at each object, such as the broom or the cloth,
and each of her movements is attained with rectitude and finality.
The humor stems from the variance between her rationally oriented
attitude and her unconscious activities. The servants, and later Patricia, observe her antics while holding back their laughter—and
their fright. They are concerned for her sanity. Xantus comments
that she reminds him of a specter.

> Xantus: And this is what has taken place every
>   day since our master forbade her to do
>   the household chores.
> Minna: Are you certain she is only making believe?
> Xantus: Making believe? Of what?
> Minna: Of being a ghost? (p. 272).

In Crommelynck's hands, Balbine's somnambulism is comic, ordered, and in perfect keeping with her ideations. She who demands
obedience from all those around her is herself the target of the
irrational. In this sense she may be looked upon as a takeoff on Lady
Macbeth's sleepwalking and the disorder present in her unconscious. "This kind of woman," wrote the critic Marianne Stoumon
about Balbine, cannot stand "man or nature" and thus "substitutes
principles and rules" for life itself.[13]
    Her sense of morality is made to look ridiculous, too. She sees
only vulgarity in friendship, degradation in sex, and refuses to share
a bed with her husband. Her attitude clearly corroborates
Baudelaire's statement concerning laughter: "It is intimately linked
to the accident of the ancient fall, to physical and moral degrada-

tion."[14] Olivier, a robust, healthy, and joyful man, accepts his wife's commands at first because she convinces him that her reasoning is right.

> Later, I'll be the one to ask you to give me a child: "My very dear Olivier, give me a child." But until that time we will each have our separate rooms. You must admit, I'm right. You are always too hot when I put on a blanket; and I'm shivering. I lie down in the shape of a capital G, you in the X position: these two letters do not fit into monogram form (p. 207).

One of the most humorous scenes in the entire play—worthy of *Lysistrata* or *Amphitryon* because of the sexual innuendoes—is Balbine's encounter with the village whore, La Faille. Balbine wants to buy some adjoining property owned by La Faille. A short and stout woman in her forties, La Faille enters richly dressed, made up to the hilt, with curly blond hair, and wearing ample jewelry. Her speech and her looks are not really vulgar and Balbine does not suspect that she is not a morally upright person. La Faille, therefore, introduces an element of ambiguity into the proceedings. At first, she seems to mirror Balbine's philosophy. She is economical and understands the value of money because she has worked hard her entire life, "never having wasted a penny" and she is "orderly" and "reasonable" (214). When talking about her life, however, her language is so ludicrous as to be on a par with the best of Molière and Beaumarchais. She blends elegance with slang and puns with intellect, shocking the prudish Balbine with her choice of words.

When she was fifteen, she confesses, she was walking head high one day on a country road, proud of her looks and body. Someone called to her. It was farmer Lambert. He accused her of having stolen something and hiding it under her dress. He asked her to follow him into his house so he could find the article. Instead, he discovered other joys. He gave her a present and told her that each time he saw she had not stolen something, he would give her money. One thing led to another and La Faille became a wealthy woman, sought after by some of the most intriguing men. At the end of La Faille's speech, Balbine faints and Olivier rushes in. After her recovery, Balbine tells her husband to treat her with kid gloves, her "heart is too small to stand the least bit of emotion without weakening" (p. 216). The next moment, in a burst of anger, she orders La Faille to leave and never to return.

I want her to leave this region; let her bed be burned right where it is (p. 217).

Sometime later, after Balbine's attempts to purchase the land have failed, La Faille is recalled, thus placing economics over morality. And La Faille injects a well-placed saying:

He who tires himself by spying on his neighbor is blind as to the goings on in his own home (p. 251).

La Faille states she is a simple and straightforward woman; she has no secrets and is far more pleasant a person than Balbine with her highbrow notions, her clockwork precision, and her slave-driver mentality. To some degree, La Faille is reminiscent of the Romantics' conception of the redeemed prostitute whose heart is in the right place, as in Victor Hugo's *Marion Delorme* or Dumas' *The Lady of the Camelias*. Kinder than Balbine, La Faille helps Olivier at the end to resort to his ruse, thus right a wrong. It is La Faille, too, who teaches Balbine the lesson of life.

Although dictatorial but not vicious, Balbine acts within the framework of her limited upbringing. Banter and humor have been banished from her world since she was brought up with a negative understanding of the Protestant ethic: labor has sure reward. Only when Olivier senses real danger to his household does he begin to take things into his own hands.

She cannot lie. She is a standing lie . . .
She is the innocent liar. She is unaware of the truth of men and of life. Her virtues are not rooted in love.
Her wisdom is sterile! She understands everything and feels nothing!
She forces me to degrade myself by plotting drunkenness (p. 308).

Olivier finally realizes that everything about Balbine is a sham and he cannot live with it. He therefore must resort to some outrageous plan that will shock her into a new frame of reference. No longer sheepish, he decides that fortitude is the best policy.

Balbine stems from a long history of satiric types in comic French theater. In medieval farces, for example, this kind of woman has been ridiculed. In *The Happy Sermon Concerning the Evils of Marriage*, matrimony is represented as a veritable inferno; in *Colin's Farce*, the wife is jealous, quarrelsome, and materialistic. One searches in vain in medieval farces for the discreet, submissive, and wise wife. The moral of many of those farces is quite the contrary: "If one could change wives the way one changes mules . . ."; but the question was, What would be gained? Perhaps the second would be worse than the first. In *The Lover's Farce* the man married to the unfaithful but clever and discreet woman turns out to be far happier than the husband whose wife is an irreproachable mate and a big crank. The "virtuous" but "unbearable" woman is a high price for any man to pay.

The audience's sympathy goes to the love-sick Patricia. Misunderstood by her stepmother, virtually ignored by her newly married father, she is the only one in the play whose fantasy life dominates. Like Giraudoux's Isabelle in *Intermezzo*, Patricia lives intensely in her world of make-believe. Her Italian lover has become reality for her, an indication of her desperate need for companionship and love. Patricia is just emerging from the child's realm to that of womanhood. Unaware of evil in the world, she cannot understand why Balbine castigates her. Why should she be a wronged girl, degraded and forever ruined? When the truth of her dreamworld is revealed, Balbine comes to accept the fact that the entire situation has been trumped up. Patricia is happy to accept Gabriel as her mate.

It is Patricia's wonderfully fresh nature that gives her charm. She is ready to give affection and to accept it. Both she and Isabelle are unspoiled and timid; each delineated with expertise. They are not comic but poetic characters, highly romantic beings who shudder at the least thought of a Prince Charming and smile with glee when they learn that their wildest hopes have been realized. Their love is pure and their ways tender, their understanding of human nature deep. They are refreshing in their sincerity and candid in their relationships, in sharp contrast to Balbine's stern puritanism. Crommelynck succeeded with felicity in capturing their various moods: joy, disappointment, and melancholia. Certain traits of character may have been modeled after the tender Marie Soderini and Catherine Ginori in Musset's *Lorenzaccio*. However, unlike the worlds of these women which were shattered, Patricia's and Isabelle's become joy incarnate.

Particular attention must be paid to the servants. Their sobriety and their disdain are exaggerated and thus rendered absurd. They are rustic characters, outspoken, frank, and natural, similar to Shakespeare's buffoons and also resembling Molière's servants. They stand for common sense and are in keeping with Molière's dictum on the subject: that common sense and naturalness are the best guarantees in life against being pedantic and the best manner of enjoying existence.[15]

Xantus and Minna indulge in sarcasm and puns; they mock and jeer everything society has superimposed on man. Playful and enjoying each other's company, they look upon life as a happy experience and their work as play. Their chiding, in the manner of Punch and Judy, becomes a vehicle for entertainment, their ribald humor a collective social phenomenon.

Minna: Half or even a quarter of my work would exhaust you.
Xantus: Would be enough to exhaust me? Now you're the one whose lying, that's it.
Minna: I'm lying. And if lying had an odor, the entire country would smell; you'd be heard through the nose (p. 170).

No class satire is aimed at in connection with Xantus and Minna; rather, the humor resulting from Balbine's monoview of family life is juxtaposed with the relatively healthy attitude of the other protagonists. The servants are modern versions of traditional farce types: their vocabulary is rich and succulent; it is made up of borrowed words, patois, and neologisms. Their insults and the slaps and kisses each metes out to the other give the effect of low-geared comedy. They are composites, yet individuals, episodic characters that help unmask what is natural in life. They underscore morality through misadvanture.

Balbine's ultramoral viewpoint has led Minna to become a *voyeuse*. She spies on Patricia "to see if she is in bed, sitting, or standing up" (p. 73). Her reasons for spying are so innocuous that they become ridiculous. The enforced emotional blockage Balbine's moral restrictions have placed on the servants have made them vindictive and dishonest. Minna accuses Xantus of having had an affair with the laundress. As punishment for his unbridled sexuality, Balbine forces him to marry Minna (p. 245). Xantus has begun to lie about household funds and keep the money he should have spent on lumber (p. 202). Minna tries to instill fear in him, declaring that he will go to prison for sure. He answers quite nonchalantly:

No, I'll not go to prison! I'll drown myself first and then I'll hang myself and I'll poison myself with mushrooms. And it will really be too bad because my mother is still alive. And the poor dear old woman will say: "Xantus has stolen my turn! Xantus has made me sterile to the end of the centuries! (p. 202).

Each time Minna appears onstage, Balbine reprimands her for her décolleté and short skirts. At first, Minna answers with pride: "I have quite something under my dress," a retort that makes Balbine stagger with shock and collapse.

The scenes in *A Woman Whose Heart Is too Small* are well-knit. No one sequence is superfluous. Each fleshes out the activities, points up the characterizations, and adds dynamism to the proceedings. The dialogue is also well etched. The style is energetic and increases the flow and rapidity of the events. The vocabulary is bold and the language always appropriate to the personalities. The play is diversified in form, including comedy, fantasy, and elements of the farce. A blend of truth and artifice, *A Woman Whose Heart Is too Small* is personal theater, never outrageously exuberant but rather contained and controlled in the manner of Musset's living-room comedies. It is caricature, a tool used from Crommelynck's own aggressions, mockery, and bent for disdain. The excesses he depicts are expressions of overreaction designed to discredit love, human relationships, and man's vulnerability. Paul Klee's definition of comedy could be applied to *A Woman Whose Heart Is too Small*: "A laugh is mingled with the deep lines of pain,"[16] except that the outcome leads to guffaws, not tears.

When André Berger labeled *A Woman Whose Heart Is too Small* the "most moderate, the most contained, the most classical of Crommelynck's works,"[17] the dramatist retorted vociferously, maintaining that all of his plays were conceived along Classical lines.

Why do you speak to me of a lack of moderation? My plays are constructed with the rigorousness of Racine's tragedies. Only, I mask the construction. I want people to have the feeling that the work is in a constant state of creation, of an improvisation. But in my plays there isn't a sentence, nor a retort, nor a useless word. I am accused of piling up adjectives: there isn't one. The result is a geometric construct. Now, for example: I never write on my manuscript: Scene I, Scene II. When I finished *A Woman Whose Heart Is too Small*, I amused myself by counting the scenes: there are nineteen per act. Is that equilibrium or not?[18]

CHAPTER 9

Conclusion

ALTHOUGH Crommelynck's literary output is meager, his contribution to the theater is significant. *The Sculptor of Masks* is important in its use of the carnival spirit and the mask as a means of expelling mass anger, mass hysteria, and mass frenzy. This play is important also as a transposition of art: stage figures are transformed into weird Ensorian and Goyaesque apparitions that peer out from all corners of the proscenium, their grimacing, gargoylelike features inspiring terror and hilarity in the hearts of the onlooker. *The Puerile Lovers* introduces unforgettable characterizations: the grotesque, amnesic, and senile Baron Cazou; his wife, Elisabeth de Groulingen, who glides through her scenes like a fantasm emerging from a schizophrenic realm, and whose drollery and pathetics result from her inability to face the aging process; and a young couple who end their lives because of an overidentification with their elders. *The Magnificent Cuckold* is the best farce since Molière's. It is superior to Jarry's *King Ubu* because of its daring characterizations, the imaginative play of its ribald situations, and its incredible use of the phallus as an instrument of delight and destruction. The depiction of obsessive jealousy and the powerlessness of reason when under the sway of emotion is remarkable. In *Golden Tripe* we see avarice at work: gold inherited, coveted, eaten, excreted, and gold killing. Gold in this play is but a symbol of man's fundamental lust and overwhelmingly aggressive nature; of his compulsion to possess, to dominate, and to kill for material goods. *Carine* is a superb study of sexual anomalies; of the ingenue who so erroneously and sadly has been brought up to believe that the world is made up of sincere and ethical people; that marriage is based on love and understanding;

147

that parents are positive and fulfilled individuals who instill feelings of well-being in their children.

Crommelynck's characters are for the most part divested of feelings. They are puppetlike in their crudeness and brutality, mechanical and rigid in their automatism. They destroy traditional values; they point up mankind's stupidity and ugliness through those marvelous devices known as laughter and humor. Laughter is ambiguous, ambivalent, complex. It covers a multitude of emotions. It may be destructive, denigrating, and a means of pointing up one's own superiority. It may be derisive, witty, cajoling, shocking, and maddening, a release for some morbid psychological condition. Laughter, wrote Baudelaire, "is the perpetual explosion of [man's] anger and [man's] suffering."

Crommelynck's theater is filled with cowards, misers, hypocrites, liars, and knaves who, because of their governing passions, are ridiculous and absurd, and therefore comic. The laughter they elicit and the humor of their activities onstage may arise from feelings of discomfort, fear, and/or surprise. "Humor," to Freud, "gives pleasure by permitting momentary gratification of some hidden and forbidden wish, while anxiety that normally causes inhibition of the wish is reduced." Humor and laughter may express hostility or malice. At times they are aggressive and regressive forces. Crommelynck's humor, with the resulting laughter, is all these things. It is also exciting and stimulating. In *The Theatre and its Double*, Antonin Artaud wrote what may well apply to Crommelynck's plays: "The theatre, like the plague . . . releases conflicts, disengages powers, liberates possibilities, and if these possibilities and these powers are dark, it is the fault not of the plague nor of the theatre, but of life."

Notes and References

Chapter One

1. Fernand Crommelynck, "Un matin au Vésinet,"*Maurice Utrillo.* Paris: J. Foret, 1956, 37.
2. Jeanine Moulin, *Fernand Crommelynck.* Bruxelles: Palais des Académies, 1974, 271.
3. Suzanne Lilar, *The Belgian Theater Since 1890.* New York: Belgian Government Information Center, 1962, 16.
4. *Ibid.*
5. Claire Dehon, "Le Théâtre de Verhaeren, Quelques interprétations." *Le Flambeau.* Numéro 1, 1975, 13–15.
6. 18.
7. "Clématyde," *En Art,* novembre-décembre, 1906. "La Maison des hiboux, *Album du ler mai,* 1913. "L'Ouragan," *L'Avenir,* janvier 22, 1919.
8. *Paris-Matin,* 6, 24, 27.
9. *Comoedia,* 6, 17, 27.
10. *Ibid.*
11. "Interview with Roger Blin," June 18, 1976 (unpublished).
12. *Comoedia,* 2, 19, 44.
13. *Ibid.*
14. Lilar, 6.
15. James Feibleman, *In Praise of Comedy.* New York: Russell and Russell, 1962, 19.
16. Lilar, 14.
17. Félix Gaiffe, *Le Rire et la Scène française.* Genève: Slatkine Reprints, 1970, 136.
18. Eugenè Ionesco, *Notes et Contre-Notes.* Paris. Gallimard, 1966, 61.
19. Wylie Sypher, *Comedy.* New York: A Doubleday Anchor Book, 1956. Henri Bergson, "Laughter," 63, 71 in Feibleman's book.
20. Blin Interview. Moulin, 11.

Chapter Two

1. Fernand Crommelynck, *Le Sculpteur de Masques*. Bruxelles: E. Deman, 1908 (Lettre-Préface by Emile Verhaeren).
2. *The Sculptor of Masks* was first written as a one-act drama in verse.
3. Henri de Régnier, "La Semaine dramatique," *Feuilleton du Journal des Débats*, 13 février, 1911.
4. Verhaeren "Lettre-Préface."
5. Régnier, "La Semaine dramatique."
6. Verhaeren "Lettre-Préface."
7. Jeanine Moulin, *Fernand Crommelynck*. Brussels: Palais des Académies, 1974, 49.
8. Paul Haesaerts, *James Ensor*. New York: Harry Abrams, 1959, 84.
9. 88.
10. 163.
11. Oscar Cargill, Brullion Fagin, William Fisher, *O'Neill and his Plays*. New York: New York University Press, 1963, 116.
12. André Berger, *A la Rencontre de Fernand Crommelynck*. Paris: Sixaine, 1946, 9.

Chapter Three

1. Charles Baudelaire, *Oeuvres complètes*. Paris: Gallimard, 1961, 981.
2. James Feiblemen, *In Praise of Comedy*. New York: Russell and Russel, 1962, 88.
3. *The Reader's Encyclopedia of World Drama*. New York: Thomas Y. Crowell, 1969.
4. Henri Bergson, *Le Rire*. Paris: Presses Universitaires de France, 1960, 4, 5, 20.
5. André Breton, *Anthologie d'Humour Noir*. Paris: Jean-Jacques Pauvert, 1966, 221.
6. Allardyce Nicoll, *Masks, Mimes and Miracles*. New York: Cooper Square, 1963, 69.
7. *Eugene O'Neill and his Plays*. New York: New York University Press, 1963.
8. Told to me by Roger Blin. June 16, 1976.
9. Sigmund Freud, *The Basic Writings*. New York: Random House, 1939, 77.
10. Marcel Lapierre, *L'Atelier*, 9, 13, 41.
11. Robert Kemp, *Le Monde*, 1, 22, 46.
12. Guillot de Saix, 9, 10, 21.

13. Sandor Lorand, *Perversions.* New York: Grammercy Books, 1956.

14. Esther Harding, *Psychic Energy.* Princeton: Princeton University Press, 1973, 242.

15. *Actors on Acting* (edited by Toby Cole). New York: Crown Publishers, 1949, 441.

16. Vsevolod Meyerhold, *Le Théâtre théatral.* Paris: Gallimard, 1963, 171.

17. *Encyclopédie du Théâtre contemporain.* Paris: Olivier Perrin, 1959, 28.

18. Meyerhold, 155.

19. 157.

20. 159.

21. *L'Oeuvre,* 18 septembre, 1941; *Paris-Midi,* 6, 9, 41; *L'Atelier,* 9, 13, 41.

Chapter Four

1. Jeanine Moulin, *Fernand Crommelynck.* Brussels: Palais des Académies, 1974, 53.

2. *Gaston Baty et le renouvellement du théâtre contemporain.* Paris: Association des amis de Gaston Baty, 1966, 21.

3. Paul Surer, *Le Théâtre Français contemporain.* Paris: Société d'Edition d'enseignement Supérieur, 1964, 45.

4. Pierre Macabru, *Arts,* 4–10, avril, 1956.

Chapter Five

1. Bettina Knapp, *Louis Jouvet: Man of the Theatre.* New York: Columbia University Press, 1956, 99.

2. C. G. Jung, *The Psychogenesis of Mental Disease.* New York: Pantheon Books, 1960, 56.

3. 56.

4. 45.

5. 33.

6. Charles Baudelaire, *Oeuvres complètes.* Paris: Pléiade, 1961, 981.

Chapter Six

1. René Malamud, "The Amazon Problem." *Spring,* 1971, 1–19.

2. Allardyce Nicoll, *Masks, Mimes and Miracles.* New York: Cooper Square, 1963, 160–70.

3. 164.

4. Oto Bihalkin-Merin, *Great Masks*. New York: Harry Abrams, 1971, 97.

5. Agalin Gheerbrant, *Dictionnaire des symboles*. Paris: Seghers, 1973, 127.

6. *Encyclopédie du théâtre contemporain* I. Paris: Les Publications de France, 1957. 49.

7. 50.

8. Gertrude R. Jasper, *Adventure in the Theatre*. Rutgers: Rutgers University Press, 1947, 270.

Chapter Seven

1. Paul Achard, *Ami du Peuple*, 22, 11. 1934.
   Gérard Bauer, *Nouvelles Littéraires*, 24, 11. 1934.
   Pierre Brisson, *Figaro*, 3, 12. 1934.
   Pierre Lièvre, *Jour*, 22, 1. 1934.
   Emile Mass, *Petit Bleu*, 22, 1. 1934.

2. Jean Guignebert, *Libération*, 22, 11. 1956.
   Robert Kemp, *Le Monde*, 22, 11. 1956.
   Max Favalelli, *Paris Presse*, 23, 11. 1956.

3. André Breton, *Anthologie de l'Humour noir*. Paris: Pauvert, 1966, 16.

4. *The Basic Works of Aristotle*. New York: Random House, 1941. *Poetics*, 5.

5. Eugène Ionesco, *Notes et Contre-notes*. Paris: Gallimard, 1966, 61.

6. Lionel Casson, *Masters of Ancient Comedy*. New York: Minerva Press, 1960, 67.

Chapter Eight

1. Nicoll Allardyce, *The Theatre and Dramatic Theory*. New York: Barnes and Noble, 1962, 125. (quoted from "The Argument of Comedy" by Northrop Frye.)

2. *Comoedia*, 17, 1. 1934.

3. *Matin Belge*, 13, 1. 1934.

4. *Ibid*.

5. Wylie Sypher, *Comedy*. New York: A Doubleday Anchor Book, 1956, 13.

6. 10.

7. xiii.

8. Félix Gaiffe, *Le Rire et la scène française*. Genève: Slatkine reprints 1970, 2.

9. Sypher, xiv.

10. 6.

11. *Aristotle on the Art of Poetry* (translated by Ingram Bywater with a preface by Gilbert Murray). Oxford: At the Clarendon Press, 1945, 33.

12. Marianne Stoumon, "Crommelynck au Théâtre National," *Le Flambeau*, 38ème année, 1961, 592.

13. Charles Baudelaire, *Oeuvres complètes*. Paris: Pléiade, 1961, 978.

14. Gaiffe, 46.

15. *Ibid.*

16. Sypher, 194.

17. André Berger, *A la Rencontre de Fernand Crommelynck*. Paris: La Sixaine, 1946, 29.

18. *Ibid.*

Selected Bibliography

PRIMARY SOURCES

Carine ou la Jeune fille folle de son âme. Paris: Emile-Paul, 1930.
Chacun pour soi. Brussels: Revue Générale, 1907.
Chaud et Froid ou l'Idée de Monsieur Dom. Paris: Fayard, 1936.
Clématyde. En Art. novembre-décembre 1906.
Le Chevalier de la lune ou Sir John Falstaff de William Shakespeare. Paris: La Nef, 1954.
Le Cocu Magnifique. Paris: La Sirène, 1921.
La Maison des Hiboux. Album du ler mai 1913. (En l'honneur de la grève générale.) Bruxelles: Presse Socialiste, 1913.
Le Marchand de Regrets. Brussels: Alde, 1916.
Le Sculpteur de Masques. En Art. février 1906; mars-avril 1906; mai-juillet 1906.
Le Sculpteur de Masques. (Lettre-préface d'Emile Verhaeren.) Bruxelles: Deman, 1908.
Les Amants Puérils. Paris: La Sirèn, 1921.
Miroir de l'Enfance. Paris: *Les Oeuvres libres.* no. 145. juillet, 1933.
Monsieur Larose est-il l'Assassin? Bruxelles-Paris: Editions de La main jetée, 1950.
Nous n'irons plus au bois. Bruxelles: Le Thyrse, 1906.
Tripes d'Or. Paris: Emile-Paul, 1930.
Une Femme qu'a le coeur trop petit. Paris: Emile-Paul, 1934.
"Un matin au Vésinet," *Maurice Utrillo.* Paris: J. Foret, 1956.

Plays

Théâtre I. I. Paris: Gallimard, 1967.
    Le Cocu Magnifique
    Les Amants Puérils
    Le Sculpteur de Masques

Théâtre II. II. Paris: Gallimard, 1968.
>   *Tripes d'Or*
>   *Carine*
>   *Chaud et Froid*

Théâtre III. Paris: Gallimard, 1968.
>   *Le Chevalier de la lune ou Sir John Falstaff de William Shakespeare*
>   *Une Femme qu'a le coeur trop petit*

Plays that have not been located and perhaps were never written:

L'Ange qui pleure, Le Chemin des Conquêtes, Le Coeur volant, Maison Fondée en 1550, Le Cimetière de belles amours, La Gourgandine, Va mon Coeur.

SECONDARY SOURCES

BATY, GASTON. *Le Masque et l'Encensoir.* Paris: Librairie Bloud et Gay, 1926. *Rideau Baissé.* Paris: Bordas, 1948. (Fine analyses of Baty's art.)

BELLESSORT, ANDRÉ. *Le Plaisir du Théâtre.* Paris: Perrin, 1938. (Good picture of French theater.)

BERGSON, HENRI. *Le Rire.* Paris: F. Alcan, 1900.

BERGER, ANDRÉ. *A La Rencontre de Fernand Crommelynck.* Liège: La Sixaine, 1947. (Inadequate summing up.)

BLANCHART, PAUL. *Gaston Baty.* Paris: Nouvelle Revue Critique, 1939. (Good analyses.)

BLOCH, JEAN-RICHARD. *Destin du théâtre.* Paris: Gallimard, 1930. (Interesting panoramic view.)

BRETON, ANDRÉ. *Anthologie de L'Humour noir.* Paris: Edition du Sagittaire, 1940.

COGNIAT, RAYMOND. *Gaston Baty.* Paris: Les Presses littéraires de France, 1953. (Interesting study.)

CORNFORD, F. M. *The Origin of Attic Comedy.* London: Edward Arnold, 1914. (Brilliant study.)

DEHON, CLAIRE, "Le Théâtre de Verhaeren, quelques interprétations," *Le Flambeau,* numéro 1, 1975. (Recommended analyses of Verhaeren's theater.)

FÉAL, GISÈLE, *Le Théâtre de Crommelynck. Erotisme et spiritualité.* Paris: Minard, 1976. (Excellent doctoral dissertation. Freudian analyses of Crommelynck's plays.)

FREUD, SIGMUND. *Wit and Its Relation to the Unconscious.* New York: Moffat, Yard, Co. 1916.

FEIBLEMAN, JAMES. *In Praise of Comedy.* New York: Russell and Russell, 1962. (Excellent study on comedy.)

GAIFFE, FÉLIX. *Le Rire et la Scène française.* Genève: Slatkine reprints, 1970. (Factual account of plays dealing with laughter and humor.)

GORIS, JEAN-ALBERT. *Du Génie Flamand.* Brussels: Raymond Dupriez, 1945. (Excellent and precise work.)

GROSSVOGEL, DAVID. *The 'Self-Conscious Stage in Modern French Drama.* New York: Columbia University Press, 1958. (Fine study.)

IONESCO, EUGÈNE. *Notes et Contre-Notes.* Paris: Gallimard, 1966.

LEVINE, JACOB. *Motivation in Humor.* New York: Atherton Press, 1969. (Psychoanalytical study.)

LILAR, SUZANNE. *The Belgian Theatre since 1890.* New York: Belgian Government Information Center, 1950. (Very general work.)

LUGNÉ-POË. *La Parade. Acrobaties.* Paris: Gallimard, 1931.

———. *La Parade. Le Sot du Tremplin.* Paris: Gallimard, 1930. (Important works.)

McCOLLOM, WILLIAM. *The Divine Average.* Cleveland: Western Reserve University, 1971. (Excellent study of comedy. Highly recommended.)

MOULIN, JEANINE. *Fernand Crommelynck.* Bruxelles: Palais des Académies, 1974. (An Anthology of Crommelynck's unpublished works.)

ROBICHEZ, JACQUES. *Lugné-Poë.* Paris: L'Arche, 1955. (Interesting insights on Lugné-Poë's contributions.)

SYPHER, WYLIE. *Comedy* New York: A Doubleday Anchor Book, 1956. (Very helpful work.)

SOLVAY, LUCIEN. *Le Théâtre Belge d'expression française* depuis 1830. (Excellent.)

SURER, PIERRE. *Le Théâtre français contemporain.* Paris: S.E.D.E.S., 1964. (A classic of its kind. Gives a panoramic view of modern French theater.)

Index